# The Commandos

Donald Gilchrist was commissioned into the Cameronians (Scottish Rifles) TA and was called up at the outbreak of war in September 1939. He volunteered for special service in the commandos, completed the commando course at Achnacarry in the Highlands of Scotland and was retained as instructor before being sent to No. 4 Commando in time to take part in the assault of the German Gun Battery at Varengeville, the Dieppe Raid. It was as an adjutant that he landed on the Normandy beaches on D-Day. He later became second in command of the unit in Germany.

Donald Gilchrist is a member of L'Association Franco Britannique, and the Franco-Scottish Society. He is now retired and lives with his wife in Ayr. He plays golf and enjoys painting in oils. He is the author of *Castle Commando*.

# The Commandos
## *D-Day and After*

DONALD GILCHRIST

ROBERT HALE · LONDON

© *Donald Gilchrist 1982*
*First published in Great Britain 1982*
*as* Don't Cry For Me – The Commandos: D-Day and After
*First paperback edition 1994*

ISBN 0 7090 5391 6

Robert Hale Limited
Clerkenwell House
Clerkenwell Green
London EC1R 0HT

The right of Donald Gilchrist to be identified
as author of this work has been asserted by him
in accordance with the Copyright, Designs and
Patents Act 1988.

2 4 6 8 10 9 7 5 3 1

Printed in Great Britain by
St Edmundsbury Press Limited, Bury St Edmunds, Suffolk
Bound by WBC Bookbinders Limited

# Contents

6

# Illustrations

# Maps

## Picture Credits

Imperial War Museum: 6, 7, 8, 9, 10; Major Bill Boucher-Myers: 14; Bill de Lieftde: 15; William S. Thomson: 16; Scottish Tourist Board: 17; author and friends, the remainder.

This book is dedicated
to
Donald
the son of Jock McCall
and
to all the sons
of all the fathers
the Long, the Short, the Tall
who
put it to the touch
living—loving—laughing—dying
don't cry—
for a Castle Commando!

# Acknowledgements

I wish to express my thanks and appreciation to all those who have contributed and assisted me in my task and to mention very specially:

Brigadier the Lord Lovat, DSO, MC, TD, LLD, DL, JP

Major Bill Boucher-Myers, DSO

Lieutenant Maurice Chauvet of Paris

Archie Venters, a Royal Marine

Henry Brown, MBE, Secretary, Commando Association

Purdie & Kirkpatrick Ltd., Ayr. (Photocopying)

Robert M. Gardiner, Solicitor, Ayr

C. H. J. Peters, Master of Town Records, Vlissingen

L'Amicale des Anciens Parachutistes S.A.S. et Commandos, French Foreign Legion

Lieutenant-Colonel Robert Dawson, CBE, DSO

*Scottish Express* International

Sandyford Foods, Ayrshire

My wife, Rosemary Anne

# Foreword

In this exciting book Donald Gilchrist recalls some adventures "on Commando" in World War II. As an old soldier I welcome his interesting story for time flies and the clock ticks faster after we have passed middle age and start reaching for a pension! It is a sobering thought to suddenly realize that two-thirds of the British population were not born when Hitler's armies overran Western Europe.

Can we glance back for a moment? For a younger generation may not be able to visualize the dismay and upheaval, followed by the devastation that shattered so many families as well as homes. The war began badly, for Britain was totally unprepared. Few now remember that for many months the prospect of bitter defeat stared this country in the face; that before America entered the war, the English-speaking world was left to fight alone.

Forty years have rolled by since Dunkirk. As I write the introduction to this book some of the little ships that saved 338,236 British and 26,175 French soldiers (without weapons or equipment) are to return across the channel to celebrate a great rescue operation made possible by a spell of fine weather and calm sea. According to Press reports none of the original skippers or gallant boat crews will be available to re-enact that magnificent achievement. They have gone with the wind and Dunkirk itself will soon become a hearsay story. There were others whose deeds were less spectacular; brave civilians who stood to arms when threat of invasion lay heavy on the land. Most of the Home Guard who kept a round-the-clock watch (mistakenly remembered as characters in a comic television series) have also gone to their long rest.

Like their obsolete aircraft—Spitfire and Hurricane—the fighter pilots who rode the clouds and saved this country have become a vanishing band of heroes. They must not be forgotten any more than the ambulance drivers, fire-fighters, women auxiliaries, the A.T.S. and W.R.N.S., and a host of others who rose to the occasion. They also serve who only stand and wait—always an unpleasant and protracted experience.

The war intensified. There was no respite. The Battle of Britain which followed the fall of France marked a turning point in hostilities—but we did not know it at the time. During four more bloody years civilian casualties blitzed in the big cities mounted to a formidable total. On the continent (death toll apart) five million refugees wandered homeless on the roads to safety.

I will not touch upon the sea or the U-boat sinkings, Hitler's pocket battleships and the convoy system that saved Britain from starvation. Sufficient to know that the Royal Navy with Allied vessels and many an armed merchantman sailing the seven seas, successfully kept supply lines open and together proved our bulwark and our shield. The author describes some aspects of a soldier's life on the ocean wave and the commando role in Combined Operations.

I come lastly to the Army: the least glamorous member of the Forces. They say old soldiers never die. Some even become bores who refuse to fade away! This book disproves such an outrageous suggestion. In the commandos we certainly had our great moments—both raiding and campaigning. And though events tend to blur with the passage of time that same spirit of invincibility and high morale remains today as strong as ever. The keen eye and heather step are best forgotten; the swift reflex actions in which we once took pride have certainly run down and the outward symbols of declining years may be "that poor old so and so who goes about with a drop on the end of his nose and most of his flies undone".

Yet it was not always so: and I doubt if loss of memory applies to any soldier who ever saw active service in a foreign theatre of war. For, whatever his age, no man forgets another beside whom he has fought in battle and I can say—without fear of contradiction—that the challenge of potential danger and shared hardship invariably brings out the best in the human race.

The fall of France was not the only setback suffered in 1940. During the spring of that year, a hastily assembled expeditionary force was driven out of Norway. Then Mussolini joined Hitler to enter the war against the Allies. By the autumn the situation in the Middle East had reached breaking point as the Axis powers began their advance across the Libyan Desert to threaten Egypt and the canal zone.

It is easy to be wise after the event. The critics have claimed our generals lacked powers of leadership or inspiration; that they were over-cautious and imbued with a defensive outlook engendered by earlier experience of trench warfare and the defence system (so called) of the Maginot Line. I agree that many brass hats were excessively professional and, for that reason, probably unimaginative; but there were some notable exceptions. Later, new and exciting formations would show (as others had done before in Elizabethan times) that the British make the best fighters in the world and such skills apply particularly to independent and irregular operations. Donald Gilchrist has rendered a signal service in bringing to light such names as the S.A.S. Airborne Forces and Army commandos but first a halt is necessary to trace cause and effect during the 1940 "rethink period" when our country found itself both naked and ashamed.

One of my early masters, the much-loved, retired General Adrian Carton de Wiart, V.C., who lost a hand and an eye in World War I and led his men over the top in the Battle of the Somme armed with a walking stick and a bag of hand grenades (pulling the pins out with his teeth) was given command of the Trondheim Fiord expedition to Norway. He has described prehistoric thinking in the War Office and the lack of basic training among his troops as follows:

> The British were issued with fur coats and special boots and socks to compete against the cold. But if they wore all these damned things they were quite unable to move about and looked like paralysed bears! The snow was too deep to leave the roads. Throughout the long hours of daylight we were constantly attacked by dive bombers and Jaeger ski patrols dressed in white boiler suits and carrying automatic weapons who swooped down hill slopes as infantry columns struggled along the road. As far as guns, planes and transport were concerned, we had no trouble at all for such things were not available!

At this stage of the war the Germans had their tails up. They were very good and we were just beginners. To their credit the British Army showed a welcome willingness to learn from past mistakes. And the enemy had not allowed for the new Prime Minister. After Dunkirk, Winston Churchill wrote to the Chiefs of Staff:

I feel that the Germans have been right in both wars in what use they have made of storm troops. The defeat of France was accomplished by a small number of highly equipped and brilliantly led spearheads. There will be many opportunities for surprise landings by nimble forces accustomed to work like packs of hounds instead of being moved about in the ponderous manner which is appropriate for regular formations. We must develop the storm troop or Commando idea. I have asked for 5,000 of these "bands of brothers" capable of lightning action.

I will leave it to Donald Gilchrist, a man of intelligence and an early volunteer from The Cameronians (Scottish Rifles) to give his own account of the development of a corps élite who were later to become known as Special Service troops. He saw it all from the beginning—first as a subaltern, then adjutant and, finally, second in command of the men of No. 4 Commando whose deeds read like a fragment of the *Iliad*. From very small beginnings those "bands of brothers" were destined to land as shock troops on D-Day, smash through Hitler's Atlantic wall and then lead the way across Europe.

The author has spared the reader an overdose of blood and thunder. This is a human story which describes a group of ordinary volunteers—young and physically fit, who took to the sea in ships—who later became men whose discipline and dedication never failed them in severe battles against the odds. Military prowess today may have critics—this book should remind us of Napoleon's famous dictum—that bravery is never out of fashion.

Lovat

Beauly
Scotland

In the beginning . . . it was dark
. . . when we sailed

# I

## Screaming Seagulls

The sound was hellish. Blood-curdling. Loud, piercing and raucous. The seagulls were screaming—screaming for food, screaming for flesh, screaming for blood! They were swooping and whooping, yellow and white painted braves on the warpath, shrieking for scalps.

Today was 5 June 1944. The invasion of France was about to begin.

All Britain had waited for it—our Allies had prayed for it—the whole world held its breath and watched for it—Stalin and Russia were pressing for it—and now a quarter of a million men were embarked on ships prepared for it.

God willing, this had to be "it".

On the upper deck of the *Princess Astrid*, I stood at the rail and listened. The gale-force wind howled and whined about the masts and stays. Under my feet I felt the ship rise and fall on the ebb and flow, uneasily tugging at her moorings by the quay in Southampton Harbour. The hawsers tied fast to bollards creaked ominously, protesting, restraining.

Out there, beyond the reaches of Southampton Water, the sea boiled and frothed in a mad rage. Angry waves licked at the concrete groynes spitting green venomous slime and spleen. Foam and spray spilt over in fury—yet the sky was blue.

Who would be a sailor on a day like this? Not me! Then why was I here?

Simple. The Royal Navy was here. No. 4 Commando was here. As adjutant of the commando I was here. I had nothing better to do and nothing better I wanted to do.

Hands cupped, I lit a cigarette. I sucked at it, drawing smoke, injecting adrenalin. I needed it. I sniffed at the breeze and smelled the tang. Dumb with awe, I stared over the starboard side.

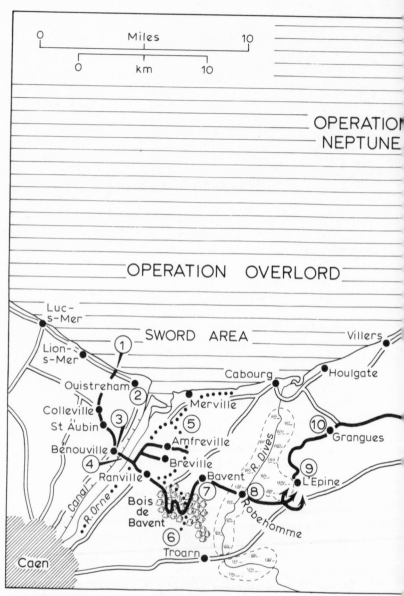

1. The Normandy Campaign from 6 June to 6 September. Movements of No. 1 Special Service Brigade commanded by Lord Lovat, DSO, MC, and composed of Nos. 3, 4, 6 and 10 Inter-Allied Commando and No. 45 Royal Marine Commando.

**Key**

1. 7.40 a.m. 6 June; 2. Assault at 11 a.m.; 3. Bénouville, the first village liberated in the night by 6th Airborne Division; 4. Crossing of Pegasus Bridge over River Orne at 4 p.m.; 5. Line of Resistance 6 June–30 July;

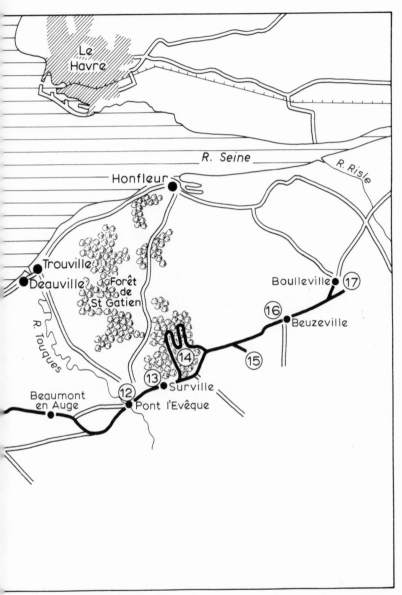

6. Position from 31 July to 16 August; 7. Capture of village, 17 August;
8. Night advance 18–19 August; 9. Attack, 19 August; 10. Graves of 6th
Airborne Division; 11. No. 1 Special Service Brigade moves on lorries;
12. Pass through town in flames; 13. Halt, 24 August; 14. Night advance,
24–25 August; 15. Rest under apple trees; 16. 26 August – first contact
with F.F.I.; 17. Reconnaissance of Honfleur and departure for England 6
September (From maps and information kindly supplied by Maurice
Chauvet, Premier Bataillon Marin Commando Français and No. 4
Commando.)

Every kind and size of ship lay anchored—battleships, cruisers, destroyers, tank landing-craft, infantry landing-craft, assault landing-craft, motor launches, motor torpedo-boats and mine-sweepers—a fleet, a host of ships, a great armada, rising and falling with the whistle of the wind and the roll of the waves. Shades of Drake, Hawkins, Frobisher and Nelson! These sailor heroes would turn over in Davy Jones's locker and go sea-green with envy.

These vessels were only part of the invasion armada. I thought about it. Five assault forces had been embarked on 4,000 ships at twelve different ports on the south coast of England. When they sailed they would rendezvous south of the Isle of Wight for the invasion of Normandy—like collecting the players in the dressing-room before the game, the war game.

Minesweepers would clear a passage through the extensive minefields laid by the Germans as the first line of their defence, while 1,000 warships would provide an escort, support the landings and pound the enemy coastal batteries with huge 15-inch guns—famous ships like the *Warspite*, the *Ramillies*, the *Black Prince*, the *Ajax* and many others.

As a bonus, batteries of 25-pounders, artillery guns made famous at the desert battle of El Alamein, had been mounted on tank landing-craft to add to the fire and flame. More batteries of rocket-firing guns, fixed on snub-nosed landing-craft, would spew and fart a murderous, sickening dirty dose of high-explosive diarrhoea.

Allied air supremacy was complete. Some 4,900 fighters and 5,800 bombers would provide an umbrella to shelter the invasion forces, in addition to bombing the German lines of communication—the vital French railway network. Spitfires and Thunderbolts, the war chariots of air heroes, would be joined by the new American P51, the Mustang. Fitted with a Rolls-Royce Merlin engine developing 1520 horsepower, the extra poke raised the speed of the P51 to 441 m.p.h., a streak of lightning to electrocute the enemy.

I heard the mumbling drone of giant bees and glanced up. Fighter aircraft were patrolling high above. I could see the ether trails feathering the blue sky—R.A.F. eagle beagles growling for a dogfight.

Elsewhere, swaying back and forward, were huge ungainly barrage balloons, like grey silken foetuses joined by thin umbilical cords to Mother Earth, giving us protection from "harbour hoppers", low-flying enemy aircraft.

What else had the boffins, thought up?

Bomber Command had been given an extra chore. They had to drop leaflets in German-occupied countries. These leaflets were designed to give hope and encouragement to those grinding their teeth in despair under the heel of the Nazis.

When the ground crew loaded the bombs manually, they used the space between the bombs and the bomb door, stuffing in masses of leaflets, tied up in bundles with string. The string was allowed to drop through as the bomb doors were closed, then it was cut. As the bomb-aimer released his explosive cargo, he also released a hail of leaflets in French, German, Dutch and Polish. To be caught on German-occupied territory in possession of one of these leaflets meant instant death. Allied boffins cooked up covers to make the leaflets look like children's bedtime story books. In this way, the people of Holland were secretly informed of the birth of their royal princess, Margriet, in Canada.

Along with these leaflets, counterfeit money and food coupons were dropped to upset the economy. It was nice to know that the Germans too were suffering rationing. But how had we managed to get the exact details of the design and watermark of the currency and coupon paper? Perhaps some of the books I had read were not so far-fetched after all—maybe we did have a Secret Service.

This operation was getting to be mind-bending. Someone up top should get full marks for low, sneaky cunning. Whoever he was, he was about to serve up a surprise *suprême* for the Germans.

Intelligence reports pointed to the fact that the German High Command was convinced that the Allied assault would be aimed at Pas de Calais. An Allied poker-playing wizard was going to twist and look as if he was bust. When we sailed, window-metal foil would be dropped off the Pas de Calais to simulate, on German radar screens, the approach of an invading armada. But the guy with the poker face had been twisting and deceiving the Germans all along. Allied aircraft had been careful to drop twice as many bombs on the Pas de Calais area as they had on Normandy.

I liked it. I liked it. Pas de Calais was miles away from Normandy and I was going to Normandy. I prayed that the Jerries were rushing to Pas de Calais. I was prepared to give them fake petrol coupons to help them along. I hoped fervently that Intelligence had got it right.

Like any other soldier in a commando, I preferred to gumshoe ashore, unexpected, on a dark moonless night, to say hello and goodbye, leaving a black-edged visiting card as a free pass to hell. I flicked the cigarette butt over the side. Torn by the wind, it drifted down and floated in the water. It would soon disintegrate in the choppy swell. Moodily, I wondered what chance had a ship in weather like this?

She was a fine ship, the S.S. *Astrid*. In peacetime she had ferried holidaymakers to and fro across the English Channel. The passengers now on board were not the usual trippers seeking the sun, continental cuisine and the blood-tingling red wine of France. In place of sleek white-painted lifeboats tightly held at the davits, there were assault landing-craft, camouflaged in razzle-dazzle, two-tone grey paint—war paint. These assault craft, in two-tone colours, life and death, would carry today's passengers ashore, forty or so to each boat.

I reflected. Yes, this bevy of beer-swilling battling bruisers would go for that. The sun, eating, drinking and making merry. With a free ticket and no need for traveller's cheques, they were not unhappy. They needed only a passport, a green beret, to show their happy breed—the commandos!

Who were they anyway, these commandos? They were volunteers recruited from every regiment of the British Army. The diamond sparkle on the cap badges of their green berets boasted their pride of regiment, of honour won and honour held.

I was not only adjutant of No. 4 Commando, I was a Scot, a "Terrier", commissioned in the Territorial Army, a rifle regiment, and wore the silver badge, the Douglas star, lovers' knot and garland of thistles of The Cameronians (Scottish Rifles).

The others came from the north, the south, the east and the west. They came in all shapes and sizes, small and tall, fat and slim. Some were good-looking, even handsome, and some were downright ugly. They came from Glasgow, Inverness, Edinburgh and Fife. From bonnie Ayr, the land o' Burns, and from the Borders. There were Yorkshiremen, Liverpudlians and Londoners, cockneys with their ears ringing with the sound of Bow Bells. Men from Norfolk, men from Sussex, Irish with the blarney. And, my God, who could understand the Welsh but the Welsh? It seemed that I was the only one who spoke the King's English.

Nobody had told me to study dialects or ever mentioned French. So why did we now have the Premier Bataillon Marin Commando Français? They had joined us nine months ago when we were stationed at Seaford in Sussex having been sent to us from No. 10 Inter-Allied Commando.

No. 10 Inter-Allied Commando was an odd unit which collected odd bodies of freedom fighters of other nations and welded them into commando troops—French, Belgian, Dutch, Swedish, Danish and Norwegians. There was also a troop of German Jews issued with false papers and identity discs. These Jews had families still in Germany and if they were caught on an operation in occupied territory, they and their relatives would receive short shrift.

The French No. 7 and No. 8 Troops, although seaborne troops, held army rank. Their leader was Captain Philippe Keiffer, tall, burly with round blue eyes. He could not control his rolling gait and walked as if he were on board ship. I got seasick watching him.

The French were with us now. Our commanding officer, Lieutenant-Colonel Robert Dawson, spoke fluent French as part of his education had been in Switzerland. A good reason for the French to join No. 4 Commando. They had come to us several months ago. Being French, they wanted to be first to reclaim their native soil and we were the cavalry, the first into the beach—second to none.

Could it be that someone high up had known how it would be and had picked us out, almost a year ago, for the charge of the Light Brigade—No. 1 Special Service Brigade? There would be guns to the right of us and guns to the left of us. In fact, there would be a helluva lot of guns, that was for sure.

From where I stood at the rail, I could see commandos in small groups on deck, playing endless games of cards, dominoes, draughts and chess. Their calm before their storm.

Rifleman Keeley was sprawled out reading, shielded by a coaming. He liked a thriller with plenty of blood and thunder. He was a cockney, tall, fair-haired, smooth-faced, with ice-blue eyes. I saw a companion speak to him. Before answering, Keeley used his thumb as a bookmark. No chance of him losing the place. He would not lose the place at any time. A cool customer was Keeley. I had been in action with him and it was nice to know he would be around.

I was stuck with them. A Foreign Legion, a rough, tough,

refrigerated bunch of bandits, fast on the draw. Types that smoothly thumbed the hammers quicker than an old-time gun-slinger from the wild and woolly west.

McCall was at my side, banging his feet and saluting. Jock McCall was my "hitman", a Glaswegian, short, barrel-chested, dark-haired with grey smoky eyes. A dour, thrawn, Pictish figure standing four-square. His elbows stuck out aggressively, a jagged Scottish thistle. I would rather argue with a runaway Corporation bus careering down Renfield Street in Glasgow. No one could call Jock a great orator like Winston Churchill. When Jock spoke, it was brief, deadly, a bullet spat from the Lee Enfield rifle he cradled as his pride and joy.

"The C.O. wants you." He retired looking exhausted.

I checked my watch and took a quick dekko at the spume streaming along the breakers. Afternoon, 1525 hours, seas running high. We would need Moses to part these waters and see us safely across our Red Sea to the Promised Land.

What did the C.O. want me for? Maybe the invasion, the whole thing, was being cancelled or postponed. If it was, the administrative problems would be brain-shrinking. We were ready. All of us were at a peak of physical and mental fitness. We were highly trained, experienced and baptized in battle. It was unthinkable that we should not sail.

Just then, I remembered the name given to this operation, the code-name which had been coined. Whoever gave it the code-name also gave a prayer. The prayer, like the code-name, was short, the shortest prayer in history, but nevertheless a prayer. I mumbled it to myself as I clattered down the companionway to the captain's quarters and my commanding officer. It was simple. It said all that had to be said. So I said it, "Overlord"!

## 2

## "Overlord"

"It's on!"

I goggled at them. The captain of the ship, a lieutenant-commander with two and a half gold rings on his sleeve, his first lieutenant, known as "Number One" and sometimes as "Jimmy the One", my commanding officer, Lieutenant-Colonel Robert Dawson and Major Ronald Menday, the second-in-command of No. 4 Commando.

It's on! What was on? The kettle? Jesus! Surely they couldn't mean the invasion of Normandy was on.

Where was the drama, this moment in time, this eve of historic endeavour? There was no excitement, no twitch of the eyeballs and no red-hot sizzling signal, "England expects every man to do his duty—Scotland expects every Jock to be a lion rampant."

Speechless, romance slaughtered, I surveyed my boots. Black polish blinked back. Wraiths of Captains Courageous faded with Ivanhoe, leaving a young Lochinvar to sail out from the west.

Number One spoke crisply, "I think this calls for a cup of tea."

Christ! A cup of tea. Tea! What happened to all the splices of the mainbrace? Was this a "rum do" or was it not? Champagne would be fine, Glenfiddich perfect, or, if he couldn't afford it, a wee pint of "heavy," a McEwans.

The word would be passed to troop leaders and to every man jack over the ship's intercom, "Hear ye, hear ye, this is your captain speaking—it's on."

I tottered after them like a Pekingese lion dog following the footsteps of inscrutable Chinese Mandarin masters.

Most of the long tables in the wardroom, the home from home of naval officers on board, were filled with customers gulping hot sweet tea and buttered toast. I cheered up. There was jam as well. Len Coulson and "Big Mac" beckoned. I sat down. Captain Len Coulson of the Durham Light Infantry commanded F Troop. He was a Geordie, a native of Newcastle. Big, broad and tough like the rugby prop forward he was. His party-piece was banging the piano ivories and bawling out the choruses of "The Blaydon Races".

Murdoch McDougall was a lieutenant in F Troop and hailed from Edinburgh where he had taught languages. He could speak German. Big Mac was big, six feet three in his stocking soles. His feet were big too, he wore a special size in army boots. He was bald with soft down on either side, not unlike a large edition of Alastair Sim, the actor.

Big Mac had shown envy when I wore my family tartan, the MacLachlan, as part of my army dress. Unable to bear it any longer, he had written home for his kilt. When the colonel saw the great expanse of bright-hued tartan covering a McDougall of that ilk, he had roared, "I'm not going into action beside you, McDougall. That thing can be seen a mile away—get it off." As an afterthought, he added, "Not here, get some trousers first."

At the tea table, Mac jerked his head at the naval officers next to him. Loudly enough to be heard all over the wardroom, he spoke to Len Coulson, "I don't much like the look of this lot."

Len paused in the act of demolishing another piece of crisp, crunchy toast, wiping away the golden butter dripping from his lips, he nodded.

"Don't reckon we have anything to worry about, Mac. That's the wavy navy. I'll bet a fiver to a pound we'll end up the creek in the Norfolk Broads playing gin rummy with Blake's Holidays Afloat."

Human naval gun-turrets swung round to give an answering broadside.

"Poor chaps, these army fellows. Strong as bulls—but not quite so intelligent!"

The crossfire went on. Number One got up and made for the door purposefully. He would do the rounds, see that his orders were carried out to the last turn of the ship's screw. I would follow him shortly.

Sealed orders kept in the skipper's care had been opened. We knew the time to sail and our place among the ships in the convoy. We knew also the name of the town we had to attack— Ouistreham, Normandy, in the department of Calvados. Interesting, but not of great importance to us. What was of vital importance to every commando was the beach, code-name "Sword", the obstacles, the contours of the ground, the buildings, landmarks and streets. Our business was to get through and eliminate the German guns. Evidently, No. 4 Commando's prowess at Varengeville on the Dieppe raid had not gone unnoticed by top-brass planners. We had knocked out the German guns then.

An army beach group from 3rd British Infantry Division was to land immediately before us and secure the beach and deal with the wire. Flail tanks weaving octopus-like chains would thresh the landmines in the field beyond the beach. We could pass through and get on with our job.

Just in case it was an airy-fairy story we were going prepared for anything. Some of us would carry bangalore torpedoes. These are long, thin, metal pipes packed with explosive, T.N.T. or plastic 808, with a five-second fuse fitted at one end. Stuck through the wire, fuse lit, it would take only five seconds to blow a gap in any wire obstacle. The landmines? Ah! Well! We would not have all day to scratch around.

From aerial photographs we had noticed that the Germans had built deep, wide anti-tank ditches round the perimeter of their gun-site. The old castle and moat idea, except that instead of filling the moat with water, the Germans had filled it with landmines.

Commandos had ideas too, new ideas adapted from their experience in climbing and overcoming obstacles, to put training into effect. We had studied the aerial photographs. Mathematicians had given us measurements worked out by simple equations. At least the mathematicians said they were simple but they foxed us. Still, we had the breadth and depth. What now?

Someone had dreamed up the idea of using lightweight metal ladders of the type used by mountaineers for crossing crevasses in glaciers in the Alps and other nightmare horrors in the Himalayas. The ladders would be easy to carry if split into sections and quickly put together by means of bayonet clips, a stud and socket arrangement.

With our training it was second nature to roll, tumble or take a dive into a deep ditch. Landmines at the bottom of the ditch were a deterrent. We would have to crawl over the ladders under covering fire from companions, deadly shots who would keep German heads and gunners under their concrete blankets.

Nearly half past four. Time I followed Number One, to look round the ship and see the troops.

On the Mess deck the scene was crowded. There were bodies in various postures among heaped equipment, rummaging through kit, playing cards and reading. Some were cleaning weapons, others were checking Mills grenades, the small pineapple-shaped bombs, the size of a cricket ball, that could blow a crater in human flesh. I admired their deftness, the care with which they handled their guns and grenades. They could do it blindfolded or in the dark. It was part of their training and necessary for they operated in the dark.

At a burst of merriment, I turned to look. One man had managed to get into a hammock. He was now upside-down in a network rope cocoon, yelling a stream of lurid curses. His pals fell about roaring with laughter.

Jones asked a question, like a stab from his commando knife.

"Sir, will it be a dry landing?"

For God's sake. Will it be a dry landing? Was that all this bunch of binding beavers could think about? Wet feet! This was the end, the very last straw. Even Lovat had caught the bug. Returning from the Dieppe raid, on the shore, he had commanded to the Royal Navy, "Come in closer. No reason why I should get my feet wet." My letters home were calming. "Don't worry, the lads of No. 4 look after me." Wet feet? No! They would never let this horrible thing happen to me. Indeed, they protected me from the hard, seamy side of life. That famous liar Baron Munchausen could not have done better.

Back on deck, the wind was snell and the seas cold and unhappy. The weather prophet had forecast that things would get better. I had no doubt that we would get there and do what we had to do. Faith and confidence is stronger than hope. On previous raiding operations, commandos had been spartan-like, lightly armed and fleet of foot, to get about and then get out.

Invasion was different. First, we had to breach the defences, assault and destroy the German gun battery at Ouistreham. Second, we had to join with Lord Lovat and No. 1 Special Service Brigade, under command of General "Windy" Gale and the 6th Airborne Division, to help "Monty", General Montgomery, Commander-in-Chief of the 21st Army Group, to take up residence in France before taking a battle tour through the Low Countries to Germany and Berlin.

For a longer stay, commandos would need more baggage. Some items would be vital. Each of us had to carry a "Bergen". These rucksacks had been packed thoughtfully and as neatly as a chief executive's brief-case for a business trip—the urgent necessities for a take-over bid. For me, these were two filled magazines and spare rounds of .45 ammunition for the Thompson sub-machine gun which was my own personal choice as an arsenic pill dispenser. As the country in Normandy was narrow lanes, high hedges and thick woods, the enemy might get very close, Therefore, I had chosen a killer spray-gun, and the .45 rounds would also fit my Colt automatic, hung in the holster from the web-belt at my waist.

We had been allocated extra ammunition. I had to carry two 3-inch mortar bombs and a canvas belt of fifty rounds of .303 suitable for Lee Enfield rifles.

I added a spare pair of boots, underclothing, pullover, shirt, two pairs of socks, one army blanket, a couple of packets of cigarettes, matches, three bars of chocolate, a few boiled sweets, pen, pencil, compass, binoculars, knife, fork and spoon. To show that I had been a Boy Scout, I slipped in a piece of string and a small jack-knife. The piece of string might be useful as a tourniquet. I rejected the commando knife usually worn on the left leg of the battle dress held by two strips of cloth. There would be plenty of knives and bayonets for incisive operations. At the early stage there would be no need for paper to issue orders. Orders would be brief, probably verbal and most likely bawled.

The "Bergen" was ready. I tried it and managed to get the filled rucksack on my back. It felt as heavy as a hundredweight bag of coal, and I felt like a humpbacked dwarf with india-rubber knees.

If this was an insurance policy for life, then it was for the long term, for after, long after. Short term, on the beach, I would be an overweight almost dead duck, waddling and quacking desperately from the water's edge, scuttling for cover. There would be no chance to do that hundred yard sprint on the sand in ten point nine seconds. German marksmen would have time to dry the tears of laughter in their eyes, take pot-shots and put me in the bag.

We were about to go over the Channel pond without the benefit of web feet. Some of us could swim, some were not too good and others boasted that they could do the breast stroke in the bath. But we would have to carry dead-weight "Bergens". I, for one, found that when I was wearing it and lay down on my back, I was as helpless as a beetle. I could not get up without rolling over and getting on my knees. If I fell into the briny with this load, I would sink without trace, a body wrapped up as tightly and securely as for a Chicago gangster's fond farewell—a concrete coffin.

Wasn't there anything pleasant, anything to give me a wee, quiet chuckle?

Well, there was one thing—the thought of all those Germans heading for the Pas de Calais, jackbooting with their pet Panzers, their favourite tank toys. They would be raising hands like traffic cops and shouting, "*Heil*". At least Hitler thought they were shouting "*Heil*", in fact, they were shouting "Hell".

They had their suspicions that these creatures, sarcastic, sardonic, satanic commandos were coming and they would bring their very own brand of hell—pure bloody hell.

It was 1900 hours and time to eat. Commandos like to eat, to drink and be merry. Why not? For tomorrow—tomorrow they would be off to Normandy.

Allied Intelligence had done us proud. It was up to us, commandos, sailors, soldiers, airmen, all the King's men, to march into Normandy, but not out again.

Tomorrow, 6 June 1944—we would do just that!

## 3

## Gunslingers

For weeks, day and night, men, guns, tanks, vehicles, the materials of war, had poured into the concentration area in the south of England, to be accommodated in tented camps. The security clamp was total—no fraternization with the locals.

The weight of these bodies and the ironmongery of war was beyond my calculation. An American soldier, a "G.I. Joe", with a brown pock-marked face as flat as a squashed pancake, summed it up. He drawled, "Suah is a wonda dis god-damned island doan sink."

Confined in a camp, we were as busy as Scouts at a jamboree. We studied maps, drawings, aerial photographs and sand-table models of the area that was to be the bull's-eye in the big target for tonight. Each and every officer and man had got down to business. Their lives, and those of their companions, depended on it. Concentration on every detail would give us cat's eyes. Each item memorized—church tower, steeple, tree-lined street, water-tower, would help us to pin-point our position.

We left camp loaded in high-powered whining army trucks. Hidden by the closed canvas flaps, we sat on wooden forms, not smoking and not talking. An onlooker would have had no clue that No. 4 Commando was here—ready to go there—in fact, anywhere—fighting fit and fit to fight.

The trucks halted at the concrete hard. The flaps were drawn back and steel pins on chains pulled out to let the tailboards clatter down. With others, I jumped down and stamped my feet. A small weight was sewn into my battle-dress trousers where they were tucked into gaiters. When I banged my feet on the ground, the

2. Sketch map of Ouistreham compiled by Intelligence Section of No. 4 Commando, as a guide. Information about beach defences and fortifications, obtained from aerial photographs, was added and the map was later used to produce a sand-table model for briefing troops about distance to objectives, obstacles and recognizable buildings. Committed to memory by commandos *en route*, it enabled them to operate without carrying maps or information of use to the enemy if they were captured.

weight drew heavily on the trouser creases to make two razor-edged lines.

Since the Vaagso, Lofoten, Boulogne and Dieppe raids, newspapers had given us rave notices. Crack troops had to be top in everything. If there was to be a competition in bullshit, it was O.K. with us, we wanted to be the best.

The ship alongside the quay had loomed large enough to venture across the channel. Naval ratings were on deck by the gangway, which dropped at a steep angle to the hard. A sailor with his cap balanced cheekily on the back of his head, shouted, "'ere Nobby, look at 'em. 'itler won't arf larf wen 'e sees this lot." Then he bawled, "Get yer 'air cut."

I chuckled as I listened. A soldier replied, "Is this yer wee boat? Whar is the paddles?"

As I went on board, there had been no shrill of the bos'n's pipe, no fanfare of trumpets, no sound of the piobh mhor. But these damned seagulls were flapping about, streaking, shrieking chillingly.

Here I was at dinner. The meal was good—soup, roast beef of Old England, for hearts of oak and men of steel. There was apple "pud" too. I stirred the sugar in my coffee, oblivious to my companions at table in the wardrooom. Thinking, worrying at administrative bones, already well-chewed by other staff bulldogs.

A nominal roll of every officer and man of No. 4 Commando who had embarked, had been completed with name, address and next of kin. They would not die unknown soldiers. Mothers, fathers, wives, all the family favourites would get the news. Companion soldiers would write epitaphs—we would remember them.

Each commando wore an identity disc. A small, hexagonal-shaped piece of hard leather about the size of a two-pence piece. On it were regimental number, rank and name. A string necklace anchored it safely, the string passed through the neat hole bored at the top of the disc and tied.

Identity discs brought out grim humour.

"What's this for, Jimmy?"

"Well, it's like this. If something happens to you, if you're blown-up like, the Adj. will no soil his lily-white hands picking up all the wee pieces—might get a bone splinter, see—very nasty for him."

"No? What'll he do then?"

"He'll pick up your disc, read your number and name, then he'll mutter, 'That's him alright, absent without leave'."

Field-dressings were vital. Each man carried his own bandage in the little pocket at the groin of the battle dress. We had received instruction from the medical officer on first aid and the use of these bandages. On our type of operation, we could not expect an ambulance and a casualty emergency ward, nor could we expect another commando to use his dressing on us. It could mean his life if he was wounded.

Last wills and testaments had been completed, torn out of the back page of pay books and carefully lodged at the appropriate department in the War Office.

Finally, last letters had been written and collected. These would be sent off after we sailed. Emotion or a careless word could break security. I wondered what they had written home to their mothers, wives and sweethearts. No lies, of course, only big exaggerated perversions of the simple truth.

Faced with a blank sheet of paper, my pen chewed down to the nib, the culture of my education at Paisley Grammar School came out. "Dear Mother, I am fine. Hope you are too. How's Dad and sister Renee? Is brother Peter still building bridges bigger and better than the one at the Golden Gate in San Francisco? He and his Royal Engineers could build a wee bridge for us here. See you soon. Love, Donald."

I did not know then that my brother, Peter, was on board ship, the *Prince David*, and that he too would land on D-Day.

A kind, generous, thoughtful lieutenant R.N. had given up his cabin and bunk so that I could rest. I pushed back my chair. There is no rest for the wicked. But I was not wicked. At least, not to those who believed in discipline, dress, demeanour and loyalty and as long as belts and puttees were blancoed white, with boots, badges and brasses beezed and burnished. If they were going to die, let them go to heaven a gleaming sight for sore eyes. Let St Peter gasp, call out the guard at the gate, to salute and present arms to the best.

To save time later, I showered, then shaved. I showed my teeth to the image in the mirror. A broken nose gave the reflection a twist and a curious knuckle at the left wrist was a man-made identification mark. Both were the scars of a duellist scrum-half in Paisley Craigielea Rugby Club, nose and wrist had been broken.

Stripped to underpants, I lay on the bunk. It was nice and warm in this cabin and I had not packed my pyjamas. Did one wear pyjamas or night-shirts in slit trenches in France? I was daft to be mixed up with this mob. I thought about them.

Captain Pat Porteous was broad, burly, fair-haired and had blue eyes. He had a habit of whistling through his teeth—like a bleep-bleep in the dark, to signal he was there. Pat had won the Victoria Cross at Dieppe, saving the life of his sergeant-major by grappling with a German about to use his bayonet. Unfortunately, his thumb was over the muzzle of the German's rifle. The German squeezed the trigger and Pat lost his thumb. Pat and D Troop were not pleased. They did not like that. They got angry and the German, in fact a lot of Germans, lost more than a thumb.

"Webby", Captain Gordon Webb of B Troop, was sandy-haired and amiable with a nice sense of humour. Before the war he had been a broker in the Glasgow fruit market. I had been under his command at Varengeville, Dieppe, Operation "Jubilee".

As the ramps of the assault craft went down, Webby was hit on his right arm by a piece of shrapnel from an enemy mortar. In the stampede up the beach, he was carried along in the wave of bodies and army boots. I had taken over to lead the first section, a small group, that managed to sneak round to the rear of the German gun-site. Like the three old ladies locked in the lavatory, the Germans did not know we were there. While I was looking at the deal, I heard his voice. Captain Gordon Webby Webb was still with us, clutching the butt of his revolver in his left hand.

Gordon had collected a Military Cross for his actions at Boulogne. He would collect another for his courage and leadership at Dieppe. You could not beat them. That was why I had joined them.

Then there was that slim, wiry type, Lieutenant Knyvet Carr. He and his troops loved the mortars, drain-pipes that spurted 3-inch bombs. Knyvet had been caught in the act of flexing the muscles in his bare torso. Try as he would, his biceps would not respond. Yet he was tough and strong with sinewy determination. "Muscles" became his nickname.

When we had been stationed at Winchester, in Hampshire, a sergeant had joined No. 4 Commando in unusual circumstances. Peter King had been a sergeant in the Dental Corps stationed on the south-east coast. He and a corporal in the same unit were inspired by newspaper reports on commando raids. Why should they not carry out their own little operation in France? They stole a rowing-boat and set out determined to win their spurs, but they lacked information, training and experience. Lost in the Channel wilderness, they got into difficulty, were picked up by an air-sea rescue launch on patrol and were brought back. Court-martialled, reprimanded and reduced to the ranks, they were subdued. Someone, however, had noticed the initiative, determination and eagerness of Peter King to lead and fight. Lord Lovat wrote to King offering him a place in No. 4 Commando. King accepted, and was now sergeant-major of E Troop.

F Troop, with Len Coulson and Big Mac, had been joined by Peter Mercer Wilson. Peter had been captain and administrative officer responsible for stores and transport. Some time before D-Day, he had gone to the colonel, Robert Dawson. Peter wanted to give up his job as A.O. and become a fighting soldier. Robert agreed but there was no vacancy for a captain. However, Peter was determined and he dropped rank and pay to become a lieutenant and section leader. F Troop was delighted. If Peter wanted to fight, he was just the chap for them.

Peter had been billeted with me at the home of Colonel and Mrs Dippie at Seaford, Sussex. At that time, he was administrative officer. There had been an air raid and the family gathered at my bedroom door while Peter shook me awake. The oracle was about to be consulted. I had sat bolt upright, as if in a trance, as he explained that incendiary bombs had hit the transport lines and set the vehicles alight. A statement of policy was due. I had given it.

"A bloody good job too! I hope the Jerries get the lot. It's high time we got new transport."

I had fallen back into a deep slumber like a Prime Minister whose conscience is clear and who has just announced a vote-catching soporific. With luck, I would be proved right and be in power for another term.

I was proved right. We got our new transport and I kept my adjutant's staff pay.

Then there was that episode with Peter Scott and his flotilla of motor-torpedo boats from nearby Newhaven. Some of us had been given the chance to go to sea with him. It was an honour to go to sea with Peter Scott and his little navy. Whether it is an honour to go out into the Channel on a plywood and cardboard boat stuck together with glue is something to wonder about afterwards. Those of us who went out had returned without having seen a shot fired in anger, but wearing such a halo of gin fumes that no one dared strike a match.

Peter Mercer Wilson went out but he steadfastly refused all alcoholic liquor. Something was bound to happen and he wanted to be involved in it. Time passed. Finally Peter gave in and went below. Naval hospitality took over and, at last, happy and bemused, Peter was tucked up in a bunk. Shortly afterwards, the flotilla had met up with some German E-boats, similar craft to those led by Peter Scott, and a battle royal took place. When the M.T.B.s berthed at Newhaven, they woke Peter Mercer Wilson and told him. He was the only commando soldier who had been to sea with them in an action—and he had slept through it all!

We had an artistic type too. Brian Mullen was a war artist well-known in Whitehall, the ultimate in London for "brass hats", high-ranking staff officers who shuffle the pawns into position on the chessboard. He was small, loosely built, chunky and had tousled hair. He was a member of the Intelligence section. Quiet, almost shy, with baggy trousers, he looked more like an artist than a soldier. It was Brian who produced for us enlarged maps and sand-table models of areas we were about to assault, with the imaginative design of that other master, Leonardo da Vinci.

There were all types, some scholars, like David Style of C Troop, former schoolmaster, slim, curly-headed and outspoken. He had led the climb up the steep gully in the cliffs at Dieppe under fire, with a character, a policeman called Jock Ennis who scrambled about in his carpet slippers.

Alastair Thorburn, brown-haired and brown-eyed, a captain, leader of A Troop, had been educated at Winchester School. When the film of Walt Disney's *Bambi* had been shown in Winchester, almost all of us had gone to see this story of a soft, kind, lovable deer. Alastair had gone more than once. For his troop, this was more than enough, they christened him "Bambi". All resemblance to the lovable deer ended there. Alastair played in a football team—a team that allowed no privileges in selection. A rip-roaring side that scored thirty-three goals in their first three games in Winchester.

He had ideas to match up to the Germans. We had information that the Germans had produced a machine-gun that could fire with the speed of quicksilver. The scholar with the hard-bitten troop had a brain wave. They got hold of a Vickers machine-gun used on fighter aircraft. Experiments were started to make it suitable for their purpose. First they sawed off part of the barrel, then they cut out a V-notch at the top of the muzzle. Soon they had a special weapon, a K gun, excreting a hot, continuous conveyor-belt of death. Round, light, metal magazines were adapted to carry 100 rounds of .303 ammunition. Two magazines were carried by each man hung at the breast like a brassière.

Nearly half-past eight. I had better get some shut-eye. I was thirsty so I got up and drank a glass of water. Now that I was up, almost ready to relieve occupied territory, I might as well go to the "heads", the ship territory where I could relieve myself. I did that and climbed back between the sheets.

The characters around me were legendary—Denny Rewcastle, Hutch Burt, Carlisle, Price, Heaynes, Howat, Macaulay, Woodward, Houldsworth and others. I knew them all. A scheming, prank-playing batch if ever I saw one.

How could an adjutant sleep with all these crosses to bear? If I had a cross to bear, which one would I prefer? I nodded to myself, I had it. What could be better than the insignia of the Free French Troops, the Premier Bataillon Marin Commando Français . . . the cross of Lorraine.

---

## 4

## French Without Tears

I really ought to get some sleep, I wanted to go on shore looking spick and span, really cool and debonair, a gallant dispensing charm as well as .45 bullets out of a tommy-gun. It was unthinkable to be a baggy-eyed corpse hearing the wail of a soldier's pibroch, "Ah canna see the target, it's ower far awa' ".

These French, who did we have here?

The French had come to Britain to be free to fight. They had arrived from many strange and outlandish places and most of them had had hair-raising, hair-breadth escapes from the clutches of the Gestapo. They had had to fight in order that they would be able to fight the big fight—for France. The moment they had waited for, yearned for, trained for, was here. A moment to remember, if any of them lived that long.

For some, the taste of victory would be bitter sweet—for their leader Philippe Keiffer, for instance. Philippe had a son and daughter in Paris. He would see his daughter again, but not his son. The lad was to be killed fighting for the Resistance, just before Philippe reached Paris.

All of them, like all of us, had gone through the mincer at the C.B.T.C., the Commando Basic Training Centre, the "School for Slaughter" at Achnacarry, the home of Cameron of Lochiel, near Spean Bridge in Lochaber, Scotland. Near, that is, if you call seven miles from Spean Bridge and eighteen blister-bulging, boot-swelling miles from Fort William.

From Paris in the spring to Fort William in the winter. It took Maurice Chauvet 882 days.

When France fell to the German Panzers in 1941, Maurice was a *matelot* on a French battleship. He decided to answer the call to freedom chimed by Big Ben nightly. Winston Churchill was promising nothing but blood, tears, toil and sweat.

After Oran, demobilized in Paris, Maurice sneaked off to Marseilles where, avoiding antagonistic, vigilant Vichy police, he joined a cargo vessel and reached French Morocco. With two Norwegians, he stole a boat and set out for Gibraltar. The epic voyage took seven days through a gale of the equinox until exhausted, starved and dehydrated, they were picked up by a Spanish fishing-boat, *El Manuel*.

Maurice and his companions were taken to Algeciras and interned and incarcerated in the infamous prison of Miranda de Ebro, there to suffer eighteen months of deprivation, with 700 others.

Maurice was a Rover Scout. Despite the horror of boils and sickness he formed a Scout troop to help others less fortunate. Dressed in rags, feet swathed in canvas and paper as shoes, he regularly held tests and kept a tally book. One day he would present it to the Scout headquarters in London, a tale of a Rover Scout's courage and spirit and a monument to the Scouting ideal which saw him through his trials and tribulations.

Eventually he was freed, although, incredible as it may seem, he had to overcome a charge for desertion in 1941 when he had escaped, a charge for which he had been sentenced to ten years' hard labour in his absence.

He reached London. Other Frenchmen, determined to join the "cause" were gathering. All were hard-bitten, experienced in the facts of peace and war. There was no red carpet for them, no oysters and champagne at Claridges, instead they were to be received at the Commando Basic Training Centre at Achnacarry. The tears, toil and sweat were now about to be suffered, the blood would come later.

Achnacarry, in Lochaber, is the home of Cameron of Lochiel. The castle is steeped in the history of Bonnie Prince Charlie. The gentle Lochiel, an ancestor of the present Lochiel, had been wined and dined at the French court. The 170 Frenchmen about to arrive would expect lavish hospitality.

The train for Spean Bridge, the whistle-stop for Achnacarry, pulled out at 0520 hours from Queen Street Station, Glasgow. Some of the French had been wakened from the luxury of a bed in the Ivanhoe Hotel. The city had belonged to them on the night before—at 0520 hours in the morning, they were ready to give it away.

At Spean Bridge there was another Big Ben—Big Ben Nevis, snow-capped and shrouded in Scotch mist. Scotch mist— drizzling, dripping, drenching, drifting rain. Raindrops would be falling on their heads, raindrops would be oozing out of the eyelet-holes of their army boots. There was no transport. Only Pipe-Major MacLaughlan and seven sock-sodden miles to Achnacarry. At Achnacarry, instead of Lochiel, there was Lieutenant-Colonel Charles Vaughan.

An Englishman! A Red Coat! Worse, a one-time regimental sergeant-major in the Coldstream Guards. Who better to deal out a hand of blood, tears, toil and sweat?

The French troops halted in the tree-lined drive to the forecourt of the castle, disconsolate, dejected and soaked to the skin. About them, men doubled to and fro over assault courses. Other men were scrabbling up a rock face clinging on by finger-nails. On the concrete square, Guards drill sergeants with pace-sticks were barking at squads like collies chasing on sheep.

Was this the legion of the damned? Well! They would be damned. They would try every tap at Achnacarry and find that both hot and cold taps gave forth cold water.

The French stayed the course. They earned their green berets and none more so than Maurice Chauvet. He completed the fourteen-mile speed march suffering, but not complaining, with a carbuncle on his heel. When they drew off his boot, the grey army sock was a welter of blood.

Maurice was an artist. His sketches and paintings do not bear his signature but a sign which speaks with sad eloquence—a wolf with a lock in its jaw.

Hotto Zivolava was a helluva name. He was an Austrian living in Paris. He changed his name to Jean Gautier, not to help my pronunciation, but to avoid Gestapo interrogation. Jean was anything but wolfish. He was more like a smaller edition of Maurice Chevalier, without the down-turn of the lower lip.

When the Germans arrived in Angiers, they told the French, "Don't worry, everything will be alright." Jean was sceptical. To his companions he remarked, "Today, there is no barbed wire. Tomorrow, there will be barbed wire." He decided to get out that night. His companions chuckled, "You worry too much."

The very next day his companions were interned behind barbed wire while Jean was on his way to Britain. It was not to be a luxury cruise. Eventually he succeeded in getting a passage to Canada. The ship was bombed and sunk in the Atlantic. Jean was picked up by another vessel in the convoy but, it too, was sunk, torpedoed. This time he was rescued from the briny by a merchant ship from South America going to Britain. Jean was put ashore at Oban, on the west coast of Scotland, in his shirt tails.

He had nothing. He was handed over to the police and locked up in gaol. An unknown picked up out of the sea in wartime had to be checked. The police were thorough but treated him well. Before being passed on to the Special Branch in London, a constable took him on a shopping spree to buy underwear, shirt, shoes, socks and a jacket—and they did not forget trousers.

At the police station, the constable's two small children, tiny tots, were curious. They toddled in to the cell to inspect the new and interesting inmate. He played games with them. They liked Jean and to the embarrassment of their father, they accepted him as their very own special friend. When bedtime came, they were adamant. Nothing would induce them to abandon their hero. If to bed they must go, then they would go to bed here, in the cell, with Jean, to suffer with him and see him through the dark hours of loneliness. Faced with such determination, the constable and his wife made up beds in Jean's cell for the children.

In London, the Special Branch were thorough. They had to be as this was wartime. A meticulous process began but finally Jean Gautier was cleared and sent to the Free French Forces.

Jean was here, aboard ship, with us. He had dared. He would win through—to France.

I thought about the medical officer, Dr Lion. A few days before, he had insisted on operating on one of his men. The latter, like most of the French, had reached Britain via a series of prison camps. As a souvenir of those days he had tattooed on his forehead the words "*pas de chance*" meaning "bad luck". Dr Lion had erased the defeatist phrase. The man with the tattoo was destined to come through D-Day and all the fighting afterwards unscathed. Dr Lion was to be killed at 10 o'clock the next day, in Normandy, while attending to the wounded.

I thought about the young French marine, hardly more than a boy, who had moved heaven and earth to get married a few days before we were sent to the "concentration camp". His English girlfriend was going to have a baby. He applied for leave to get married but was told that because of security, it would not be possible. But the French lad would not take no for an answer. He went straight to Colonel Dawson and stated his case. He explained that he knew he was going to be killed during the operation and he wanted the child to have a name. He was given his leave and he got married. He would be killed within minutes of landing on the beach, just as he had predicted.

There were others. Faure, Chausse and Boccador who had come from Africa. The three Guys—Guy Hattu, Le Comte Guy de Montlaur, who was a sergeant, and Captain Guy Vourch.

Guy Vourch had left Finisterre when he was 18 years old, to be a medical student in Paris. When war broke out, he enlisted in the French army. He sensed the collapse of France in the blitzkrieg and decided to get out. After several abortive attempts to reach Britain, he finally bought an old fishing boat in need of repair. He set himself to the task and when ready, with the help of a few friends and his brother, Yves, he sailed.

Fate struck. The engine failed and they lay becalmed. A gale arose buffeting them to and fro on the high seas. Starved, parched, half-dead, they were picked up by the S.S. *Cairngorm* off Milford Haven.

After one year in Political Intelligence, Guy applied to join the

Special Service Group and was sent to No. 10 Inter-Allied
Commando.

Guy would survive and reach Paris, marry his love, Brigitte and
become a professor of Anaesthesiolegie. Right now he was preparing an anaesthetic for the Germans. He was fixing the dose. It
would put anyone to sleep for ever. A bullet shot in a hypodermic
Lee Enfield rifle syringe, with a bayonet sharp as a needle.

Did we, or did we not, have the best people? There was a padre,
Father René du Naurois, tall, burly, bald, saintly, with round
innocent eyes. He looked angelic, but his belly showed. He
enjoyed the good life, the *cuisine magnifique*, the wine, a good
year, French, of course. What was he doing, a divine Daniel in the
lions' den?

Du Naurois was a character, a French Friar Tuck, not so rotund,
but strong, with mischievous eyes. He had been detained by
the Gestapo and Vichy Police in 1942. They allowed him to go
and he made up his mind to get out of France and escape to
Britain.

He arrived at Perpignan and contacted a doctor friend who was
chief of an asylum nearby at Cerdayne. The doctor gave him a
private room on the upper floor and explained to the nurses that
the padre was here to assist in the Christmas festivities. Each
night, when the inmates and nurses were locked up in their
quarters, the doctor crept upstairs to the padre, to tell him the way
was clear. Together they descended to the basement to listen to
the B.B.C. radio broadcast.

Christmas festivities gave the opportunity for escape. Llivia is
an enclave, part French, part Spanish. Father du Naurois, with a
Spanish priest and a Christian brother, took part in the procession
equipped with a barrel organ on top of a cart pulled by a horse.
They crossed the border in the enclave and from Cerdayne they
reached Puigcerda.

At the border there had been an anxious moment, as the
Spanish authorities checked passports. Du Naurois's passport
carried no photograph. He feigned deaf and dumb. The Spanish
priest did the talking and whisked his charges through the
barriers.

From Barcelona he made his way to Gibraltar and then Eng-
land, arriving in Liverpool. In London he met the three Guys,
Guy Hattu, Guy de Montlaur and Guy Vourch, three French
Musketeers. They convinced him that No. 1 Special Service

Brigade was the unit to which he ought to belong. That suited the padre.

René du Naurois had a problem. He had been appointed chaplain to the Free French Forces. He solved this by going back to his office and writing an order which he himself signed, appointing another in his place and transferring himself, at a lower rank, as padre to the Free French in Combined Operations.

In Normandy, the padre would insist on going on night patrol—not the safest of operations. He wanted to be with his flock of French, to attend to them if wounded, to act as a medical orderly on the field of battle. He wanted to be on hand too, to render the last rites, if needed.

Before going out on patrol and despite the padre's protests, they would whip off his woollen knitted cap-comforter, the fez-type head garment favoured by commandos, and plaster the gleaming skin with brown sticky mud. "If your cap falls off, Padre, your bald head will shine like the beacon off Le Havre. The Germans will see it from far off."

"Monty" had inspected the whole of No. 1 Special Service Brigade a couple of months before D-Day. We had been drawn up in ranks filling three sides of a square. The general arrived in a jeep. As usual, he wore a dark-blue beret and two badges—one of the general staff and the other of his tank regiment.

He stood up and stood out, sharp-faced, sharp-eyed—an eagle. He ordered us to break ranks and we instantly rushed to gather around him, hushed and expectant. We laughed at his imitation of a cocky Scot. "You are real proper chaps, real proper chaps. You and I, we'll hit the Germans for six, hit 'em for six. It will be nae bother at aw, nae bother at aw!"

I repeated to myself the piece of verse in Montgomery's Order of the Day.

> He either fears his fate too much,
>   Or his deserts are small,
> Who dare not put it to the touch,
>   To win or lose it all.

I eased myself slightly on the bunk. The credits were over for the director, the producer, the stars and the supporting cast. The next reel of film would be pure action. I would leave it until tomorrow, I was feeling sleepy.

My last letter home. I could have done better. Perhaps I should have told the truth.

The truth that, with No. 4 Commando, British and French, an association Franco-Britannique all tried, true and treasured companions, tomorrow, 6 June 1944, I would dare to put it to the touch, to win or lose it all. I was happy.

## 5

# Charge of a Light Brigade

I awoke to the throb of the ship's engines. Instantly alert, I listened to the steel plates juddering as her head rose and fell to plough the sea.

I saw his grotesque shadow moving stealthily in the doused light. My movement must have warned him, for he spoke.

"It's me, sir, McCall, brought your tommy-gun, cleaned and checked—over there, with one filled magazine."

He was a quiet man. I peered at my wrist watch. Luminous hands signalled back, after midnight, 0330 hours to be exact. The "fun" would start at 0530 hours. The guns would open up and we would go ashore.

"O.K. Jock! Sounds as though it's rough out there?"

"Better'n it was, sir. Not so choppy, more of a swell." He went on. "Time you got moving—grub's up—ah'll come back and see you later."

It sounded more like a threat than a promise.

I ran the tap, filled the basin and splashed cold water over my head, face and body. Refreshed, I towelled hard and felt the skin glow.

Dressed in battle dress, I put on my S.V. climbing boots, the type favoured by all commandos. The boots had a deep rubber tread like Michelin tyres and gave a firm grip on rock and slippery surfaces. On route-marches the rubber heels softened the deadly thump carried up the spinal cord to the brain, as boots hammered on hard road cambers. They were also quiet, soft pads for sharp-clawed cougar commandos.

I cursed the battle-dress trousers. There was not much I could do about those. But the rough, hairy, scratchy material sandpapered the tender skin inside my legs at the crotch making the flesh raw and red.

As I buckled on the ankle gaiters, ears cocked, I heard the vibrations of the ship's screws churning the water, revving as they topped a wave while the *Astrid* heaved.

The wake at the stern would be white curds and whey providing a flare-path for others to follow. Ahead in the blue-grey darkness, trawlers would be sweeping a passage through the German minefield. Bobbing up and down in the swell some guy would be muttering curses as he fumbled unseeingly with detonators. It was a helluva job at anytime, suicidal in the dark. I didn't fancy it. One mistake and for him there would be waves of goodbye. It had to be done. Nothing must impede the passage of the forces of liberation. We would owe much to a few.

In the wardroom, breakfast was being served—bacon and two eggs with lots of hot, buttered toast and lashings of hot, sweet tea or coffee. Naval officers as well as stewards served at the tables. They called this the "Last Supper". They were attentive.

"Now then me hearties, eat, drink and be merry. Oh! Don't forget to leave the addresses and telephone numbers of your wives and girlfriends. We'll look after them till you get back."

"You Navy lot aren't going to wait for us then?"

"Wait for you? How can you ask such a thing? You know our *Astrid*. She's slim, beautiful, capricious, a curvacious body. If there is any chance of *Astrid* being raped, we'll be off."

Eyes flickered to the wardroom clock. Chairs scraped back. I moved too. To Number One, I said, "Thanks." He smiled and replied, "Anytime, good luck."

Jock was in the cabin waiting. He had eaten. He was ready. He helped me on with my rucksack and I groaned at the weight. I'd run as fast as a hunchback snail with a loaded shell. Still, if we managed to get 600 men ashore each carrying 50 extra rounds of .303 ammunition that would make a reserve of 30,000 bullets.

McCall watched me go through the drill. I eased my Colt .45 automatic from its sheath to check the magazine in the butt. With the safety-catch on, I replaced it. I slid a loaded magazine into my tommy-gun. Again, I flicked on the safety catch. I didn't want to go shooting up commandos in an assault craft. McCall approved.

An adjutant had disappeared. In his place was a commando soldier, ready for the fray. There would be no time to write Part I and Part II Orders or pen sharp disciplinary notes, no time to write even a postcard.

In a raid or a battle, rank mattered little. Leadership and example in action won the day and gained respected authority. On such a day as today, every man would set his own example and fly his own personal standard. This was the day of days—D-Day—each man to his own fate.

Deep in the bowels of the *Astrid*, lights doused, we assembled to wait in silence, feeling the lift of the deck as her keel wallowed in the trough.

We had been through it all before, but this was special, very special, for No. 1 Special Service Brigade.

The Dieppe raid had been on a grand scale. But now, out there, under the cover of darkness, a fleet sailed majestically, an armada, the like of which had never been seen before. "And gentlemen of England, now abed," someone muttered. There was no chance to utter a ribald reply.

It seemed to happen all at once.

I heard the muffled sound of the ship's telegraph and the shrill of the bos'n's pipe. The ship lost way. The vibrations of the steel plate lessened.

"Hear ye, hear ye! This is your captain speaking. Crew to action stations, commandos to assault craft! And the best of luck."

Out of the corner of my eye, I saw the green light come on. The voice of Regimental Sergeant-Major Bill Morris, rapped out to slice the darkness.

"Alright, you lot, get cracking."

We moved without noise on rubber-soled S.V. boots up the dim companionways to the upper deck. My lips tasted the salt tang. I sniffed at the cold air and shivered.

Landing-craft were poised at the davits. Naval ratings stood by, a little send-off party. I chuckled at the parting shots feeling warmer with the exchange of pleasantries.

"Tell the driver to wait, my good man, I won't be a minute."

"Will I need my water-wings, Sergeant?"

"Whit ur youse chargin' fur a wee sail oan the watter?"

An N.C.O. barked, "Shut up." Moments later the L.C.A. was neatly filled, every man in the correct place. Practice makes perfect and we had practised.

I went for'ard to the bow and stood next to the colonel, Robert Dawson. We'd be the first to go off when the ramp went down.

A young naval lieutenant and his coxswain were leaning casually against the armour-plating protecting the tiller starboard of the ramp. They were wearing camel-coloured duffle coats of loose, thick, coarse, warm woollen material.

Commandos sat on fixed bench seats, one row to port and starboard and one row along the centre. It was a tight squeeze. Thirty-five men with rucksacks, bren-guns, rifles, tommy-guns, bangalore torpedoes, festooned like Christmas trees.

Usually we landed wearing green berets or thick home-knitted woollen cap-comforters. For today we had been advised to wear steel helmets, an indication that there would be a lot of jagged metal flying about. However, most commandos had a "geise", a sort of spell or taboo, and stuck faithfully to their berets "green for go".

Earlier, I had watched old soldiers pack cigarettes and matches into elastoplast tins and seal them carefully with sellotape. With the same cunning care they had stuck a piece of adhesive tape over the muzzle of their weapons. A lot of elbow grease had been used to produce the shiny, bright tunnel of light in the rifling. The adhesive tape would prevent salt or sand damaging the rifle barrel. They had ensured that the bullet percussed would find its way to the target. That's why old soldiers never die—and this lot never fade away!

There were some old soldiers in this boat. McCall was one. He was sitting comfortably behind me looking as if he was about to enjoy a trip on the *Jeanie Deans*, the Clyde steamer, to see the Rothesay illuminations.

And others. Maund, the C.O.'s batman, English, imperturbable, with his broad accent. Elsewhere in the craft would be many commandos who had been billeted in Troon, Scotland and had married local girls. Why not! Troon was in Ayrshire, the land of Burns, a famous Scottish bard, and famous for its honest men and bonnie lassies. Men like Fred Ham, a sergeant in B Troop, Vesty who had been wounded on the Dieppe raid, Macaulay, Jed Price, Ginger White and Sam Cooper. The latter was a motor-cycle dispatch rider. Before the war he had competed in the Isle of Man T.T. races.

Now all of them were about to see illuminations that would make the efforts of Blackpool and Rothesay look like a dinner by candlelight, and fireworks that would make a Guy Fawkes enthusiast give up the trade.

Some of them had been in the B.E.F., the British Expeditionary Force. After Dunkirk, they had coined a new name for B.E.F.—back every fortnight. They were going forward right now.

There was the rustle of well-greased pulleys. The craft fell away to hit the surface of the water. It slewed as the engines whirred. The helmsman fought the wheel and won. The L.C.A. veered off from the steep bulk of the parent ship towering menacingly above us.

In a few moments our craft would manoeuvre into line with others. When daylight came, it would show our presence and we'd be going all out for the beaches of Normandy, like bats out of hell.

This, then, was "it". The moment had arrived, the appointed hour.

It started with an eerie silence.

The whole world stood still, breathlessly awaiting the first night gala performance. Winston Churchill and the chiefs of staff would be in the Royal Box. He'd be smoking an outsize cigar and giving the two-finger V-sign. There were two ways of doing that. Would someone tell him to "get it right"?

I felt the soft spray on my face like the touch of Scotch mist on the top of Ben Nevis. I swayed as the craft bucked the swell, then braced myself as the old sea-horse jumped over a crest taking its fences. I began to regret my early breakfast of bacon and eggs.

Norsemen must have sailed like this, a black raven flying at the mast-head. Had this been the year 1066, Norman conquerors would have been going the other way to Hastings.

Dawn rose streakily on the skyline, pink and grey light, as the curtain rose revealing a stage and a massed orchestra with all the instruments tuned to concert pitch. The conductor would have a baton, a field-marshal's baton. He must have waved it because the music began.

A hellish cacophony of sound. A hysterical outburst of venomous clamour. Drums, cymbals, woodwinds rolled and blared as guns of the Allied fleet opened up in an ear-splitting, roaring crescendo. A storming barrage of death and destruction.

Somewhere ashore, screaming projectiles were plummeting down to raise great gouts of earth. There would be the smell of burning cordite, of scorching heat and cauterized flesh.

Those puking into the greaseproof pokes thoughtfully provided, stopped being sick, and I recovered from the queasiness I get when I smell the vomit of others.

Behind me, men crouched on the craft, poised tigers ready to spring. They were ready to follow and, like a rugby pack chasing a Gary Owen, ready to ruck, maul and tear apart any opposition.

No shout was needed. There came the searing sound of sand scraping the bottom. The naval lieutenant worked the lever. Cog teeth chattered on oiled chains. The ramp yawned open.

As one, we bounded out, splashing in the shallows, making for the beach and the barbed wire about 100 yards away. At the edge of the sand where little eddies of foam traced lace patterns, there was tragedy.

The beach group, soldiers from the 3rd Infantry Division, which had landed immediately before us, had been decimated by enemy shell and mortar fire. The few remaining were dementedly digging trenches—but in the water.

As the tidal wave of green berets surged ashore, they swept all with them—the wounded, the dying, and the half-crazed.

With both eyelids clicking like a Kodak camera, I pressed on taking mental pictures.

The beach was already a shambles of men and guns. Landing-craft were touching down. Further out to sea, wisps of smoke from the funnels of steaming ships mixed with orange and red flashes as salvo after salvo of shells was projected towards the land in a sensational pyrotechnical display.

German guns inland had taken up the challenge. Sea-water mushroomed up, craft were hit, huge explosions rocked the boats—and men died.

Brian Mullen, the artist, the gentle soldier, lay broken, dead on the soil of Normandy. He had painted many a scene, but not one like this.

In this cauldron of hell and murderous clamour, laden commandos trudged relentlessly, helping their companions, aiding the wounded. Courage, bravery, determination in action.

Half-way there, I fell on my knees. My left hand grasped a searing hot piece of jagged metal, the size of a shilling. I stared down at my chest. There was no blood and I had no pain. I heard the C.O.'s voice, "You alright, Adjutant?"

I nodded, "Yes, I'm O.K." Together we toiled on bent like half-shut knives.

We paused at the wire. A notice-board on a pole was stuck in the ground. Those we had in Scotland usually stated "Parking Prohibited", or "Trespassers will be prosecuted". This one was shorter. It was also more effective. It spelt *Minen*. Flail tanks with octopus-like chain arms were supposed to have dealt with the wire and minefields. Promises, promises!

The wire was no problem. We could stick the explosive-loaded drain-pipe bangalore torpedoes through the meshes and touch off the detonator. That would blow a gap. But who wanted to go for a stroll over a minefield? Of course, we could lift the mines and clear a passage by scrabbling about on hands and knees searching for the round metal objects. We would have to use our fingernails as detectors and as archaeological trowels, to scrape away the covering earth as gently as for an ancient earthenware discovery. It would, of course, take time and we did not have time.

Neither did that German soldier.

The German was still alive and kicking. He was throwing stick grenades, shaped like a judge's gavel—only the grenade proclaimed that judgement day was here. He was about thirty paces away, a jack-in-the-box in a gun-pit. Something would have to be done about him. He was brave. A brave German—and soon to be a dead German.

We watched as Captain Knyvet "Muscles" Carr did a little zig-zag run. His right arm curved as if bowling at cricket. We saw the parabola of the grenade he had thrown. It entered the gun-pit and exploded.

A voice at my ear muttered, "Stupid bugger."

I stared at the man and he stared coldly back. Then he added grudgingly, "The German, I mean. He's a goner."

Over on our right fifty yards from where we were, Captain Hutchison Burt of E Troop was solving the minefield problem.

Hutch was red-headed, red-faced, red-moustached and a Scot. He and Captain Alastair Thorburn of A Troop with a few others were now gingerly walking inland through the minefield, but along the wire splitting one area of field from another. This was taking a chance, but a cool well-calculated chance.

The wire which splits a minefield is barbed and fixed to wooden stobs stuck in the ground. As well as the wire strung between stobs, strands are hung at right angles from the wooden uprights like guy-ropes of tents held by wedges. It is difficult and highly dangerous for mine-layers to place mines along the wire fence. If the Germans had laid the *Teller* mines in between the wire, then . . .

We got up and followed, walking softly, the way cats do on a red-hot tin roof. We stayed close. We were through. The whole commando was through, by guess and by God.

Perhaps there were no mines. We didn't stop to find out. The answer might add to the grey hairs we'd already collected, and there were other urgent matters to do.

I did a quick check, like a worried collie. The commando was lined up in column in the right order, the French No. 7 and No. 8 Troops in the van.

I turned to find the colonel, Robert Dawson. He had gone forward to take a look-see. He was returning with blood streaming from a wound on his head. When I went to him, I received the blast of his tongue.

"What the hell do you think you're doing, Adjutant? Get them moving."

Before I could open my mouth to protest or attend to him, he glared at me and bawled, "Move, I tell you."

I moved and quickly. So did No. 4 Commando.

It was my turn to blow my top. Roaring like a bull, I bore down on the unfortunate French.

"*Allez, allez! Vite, vite! Sacrebleu!*" The French gaped at me as if I'd gone mad. Then they were as one and, with a stamp of boot and rattle of equipment, began a speed march along the route to their objective.

After the war they told me that my beautiful French commands had been taken for shouts of "Allah! Allah!"

By the high wall, on the road leading to Ouistreham, we dumped our rucksacks in the ditch. This was pre-arranged. We'd collect these later, or at least some of us would, not for the army blankets, nor for the extra pair of socks, but for the mortar bombs and extra fifty rounds of ammunition. Meantime, it was a load off our backs if not off our minds. We were now lightly equipped— spartan-like.

I turned, ready to go. Confronting me was Ronald Menday, the second in command of No. 4 Commando. He bawled. Why the bloody hell had I not sent him a message that the colonel was wounded?

Somewhere in the pit of my stomach a tiger growled. I showed my teeth and started to snarl. Bursts of small-arms fire drowned my performance. We scampered to take cover and face the personal maelstrom.

The casualties were dragged into the ditch to receive attention. Germans were shooting from a house on our right. Commando brens and rifles spat bullets to keep the Germans quiet. They could be a nuisance and cause trouble since we were in a hurry.

Just then, a tank lumbered up to stop beside us like a lost, friendly duck. Obviously the crew had been cut off from their squadron. A bit of luck for us. There was just one small snag—how to communicate in all this noise of shelling, mortaring, the rattle of small-arms fire and the grumbling of tank engines.

Someone showed me the button at the rear. I pressed it. The bell must have rung, for the lid opened. A head popped out and a voice enquired, "Was there something?"

There was. The target was described and pointed out. The tank sallied forth, halted and turned slowly. Its tracks squealed on the surface. We watched curiously.

There was no preliminary gun-fire. Instead, the crew operated a mechanism to throw a huge object like a large oil drum, a sort of aerial depth-charge. The canister hurtled through the air, turning and revolving, to strike the front of the house. There was a big explosion. The building caved in, the roof dizzily canting and spilling vermilion tiles, as if a landslide of scree on the Cairngorms.

Ronald Menday gave his brief smile. He was pleased, thank God!

From nowhere, an old Frenchman appeared, dressed in civilian clothes and wearing a black beret. He had a thin face and a drooping moustache. He seemed unconcerned with the holocaust going on around him with a detached disregard for his life. His name was Lefèvre. He and Philippe Keiffer forgot the war and embraced.

The old man was a Resistance leader in the area. Excitedly, he explained he could guide us and point out the German positions. What could be better than to have our own personal wartime Syndicat d'Initiative to show us the gun-sites, before the gun-sights saw us?

He was laughing, for God's sake! What did he have to laugh about? They told me his joke.

During the bombardment he had nipped out of the town area while the German garrison had been below ground. He had cut the cables to the gun battery and the casino, both of which were electrically controlled. He had, in fact, put out of action the German flame-throwers, the nozzles of which could have hosed a blaze of heat to cook and fry any one of us in the final assault.

Yes! I like that. It was funny. I started to laugh, but didn't get time.

As at Balaclava, with guns to the right of us, guns to the left of us and guns all about us—here came the charge of the gallant six hundred.

## 6

## Bridge over the River Orne

The balloon had gone up at 0530 hours. So we hadn't been late for our appointment with fear.

Castaways from our parent craft, the *Astrid*, we had surged ashore, toiled up the beach, gone through the wire, tiptoed over the minefield, formed up and trotted towards Ouistreham. It was light now and just after 0630 hours.

In that short period, I had seen dozens of tiny acts of bravery by men putting each moment to the test, living a year in a split second of a lifetime.

The French troops were champing at the bit, eager to be off. Grim-faced, unsmiling and resolute, they had fixed their bayonets. Steel glinted as they peeled off, going hot-spurred to their objective, the German strongpoint at Riva Bella, (Ouistreham)—the Casino.

They were ready to gamble. Men like Keiffer, Vourch, Lofi, Montlaur and Gwen Ael Bollore, to name a few, had a score to settle. They paid it, plus interest. The soil of France was at stake. In a feat of courage and gallantry they overran the German fortifications, going through the defending bodies like a dose of Epsom salts.

With a gamble, some lose. Men died with the name of their country on their lips. Among them was Dr Lion. He died attending to the wounded. He died for France. He died for freedom.

Other troop leaders were already on their way to their allotted tasks, men following, clattering behind them.

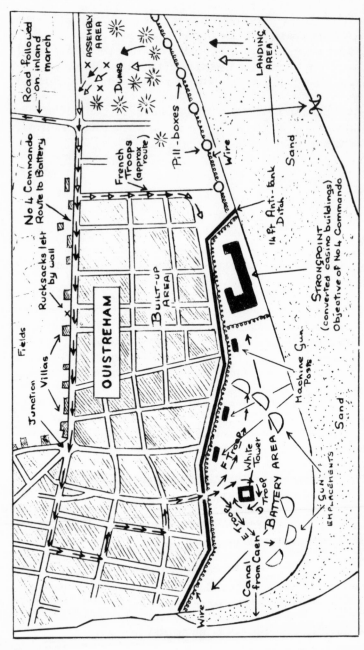

3. Assault on German gun battery at Ouistreham. No. 4 Commando's D-Day map re-drawn by Under Officer R. M. Cardwell, Ayrshire Army Cadet Force, from information supplied.

The tank commander and his men had attached themselves to No. 4 Commando. Our war was their war. They penetrated the defences at Ouistreham before being knocked out. The armour-piercing shell entered the hull and sheared off the legs of the gallant commander. A man, among men, who never counted the cost.

At the gun-site, the assault began. The old Frenchman's information was confirmed; the Germans had removed the guns inland several weeks before but the sites were still occupied. Gun crews had to be winkled out. They were. British steel, Sheffield made, flashed and winked as bayonets were fixed to extract German mussels from their shell-like bunkers.

We had not studied aerial photographs in vain. There were, indeed, huge anti-tank ditches, excavated to protect the gun-sites. The light-weight ladders we carried would be used after all. Ladder sections quickly put together by means of bayonet clips spanned the mine-filled moat exactly. Mathematical wizards at home had got their sums right. Commandos could get across.

Hidden by smoke-screens put up by 2- and 3-inch mortars, men crawled over ladder bridges under covering fire from machine-guns and rifles. Sharpshooters sniped at the oblong openings in the concrete fortresses, sending bullets to buzz inside as if stinging hornets had gone mad.

One or two, greatly daring crept up to pillboxes to post grenades through the letter-box slits. They were experienced, grasping the rifles by the left hand and using the right to unhook the grenades hung from webbing equipment. Using their teeth, they pulled out the split pin holding the detonator lever. When they let go of the lever, it would fly off and they would have four fuse-seconds to get rid of the grenade. Some counted "one" before popping the bomb into the oblong opening. The opposition would have one second less in which to throw it back.

If there was more than one slit, they went round the pillbox putting a grenade in each one. Some pillboxes were designed with separating walls inside. Grenades going in at every angle left little room for escape.

The job done, they crouched close to the concrete boxes, to await the result of explosions and flying flak inside. Cool, confident commandos muttering sarcastically, "S.W.A.L.K"—sealed with a loving kiss.

Tramp, tramp, tramp the boys are marching,
Who's that knocking at the door?
If ye dinna let us in, we'll bash yer heid and shin,
And, ye'll never see yer mammy any more!

Those Germans lucky enough to survive this onslaught staggered out, shocked and shaken to be quieted with a hail of bullets, bayonets and bombs. Others sought refuge in their rabbit-warren system of interconnecting tunnels between concrete emplacements, to wait, trapped and helpless. Their fate was sealed, hope gone, morale destroyed.

A battle of deafening noise—chatter of machine-guns, crack of rifles, whine of bullets, huge explosions. There was smoke and smog and the smell of burnt offerings permeating the air, filling the nostrils and creating a battle stench, despoiling the blue sky above.

While the sun shone, men died as shells fell from the heavens.

One whistled down to explode on the road eighty yards in front of me. A small group of men were thrown aside by the blast as if unwanted theatre puppets. Amazingly, only one man was hit. The others threw off shock and leapt to attend to their companion. Feverishly, they tore at the wounded man's battle dress to get at his field-dressing. They knew what to do and they were doing it.

They bellowed at me, "Can't you stop these effing gunners? We can manage."

Jock McCall's voice rasped, "The C.O. wants you."

We went at the double, about eighty yards and round a corner.

Ronald Menday and the troop leaders were gathered around Robert Dawson. The bandages on his head looked bloody. They were trying to persuade him to go back to a regimental aid post but he was determined to stay with us.

I reported and was informed of the situation.

The ships supporting us, a cruiser and a destroyer at call, were still firing on the German gun-sites. The naval forward observation officer attached to No. 4 Commando had been killed and his R.T. set rendered useless. Some way had to be found to stop our own guns firing on us.

The artillery forward observation officer attached to us was desperately trying to relay a message, via his headquarters on a ship at sea, to tell the Navy, "Thanks for the memory, stop firing now."

He had been with the "Desert Rats", in the Middle East. He was spitting gall. "I've seen more action with you lot in half an hour than I saw in all my service in the desert. And I was at El Alamein!"

To make matters worse, the German guns inland were firing on the gun-sites. War is a dirty business. They were firing on their own troops as well as on ours.

As I said, we were the Light Brigade, with guns to the right of us, guns to the left of us, a helluva lot of guns creating a hell on earth. Of course, bomb-aimers and gun-layers don't see the hell they've created. They live in their own little hell of sweat and toil as shells, flak and flaming tracer probe and seek—an eye for an eye, a tooth for a tooth.

I guessed that was it. To be able to take it as well as hand it out. Toughness, to grin and bear it. I bore it, but the grin didn't come through.

Menday was now to take over temporary command.

"Since there were no gun batteries at Ouistreham we could be wasting our time."

For crissake! Who in this unit got the chance to waste time?

It was estimated that the Germans numbered 200 or 300 men. Deducting fifty per cent killed or wounded left 100 or so terrified Germans with perhaps one or two hard-liners. We would leave a small force of between ten and twenty commandos to mop up, act as ferrets, snaffle the rabbits and put them in the bag. For the hard-liners, there would be a hard line—a bullet or a bayonet. The ratio of one commando soldier to five or six Germans proved ample. Those left to clean up in the following few days, prodded prisoners only too eager to go into the war cage.

Meanwhile, we, what was left of No. 4 Commando, would start the second phase—to join Lord Lovat and No. 1 S.S. Brigade, consisting of No. 3 and 6 Commandos, No. 45 Royal Marine Commando and the 6th Airborne Division, at the River Orne.

The second phase . . .

By this time people at home would have had breakfast. They would have scanned the headlines and avidly read the *Express* or the *Daily Telegraph*. The news of the landings would be out, blocked in large heavy type. The cricket scores would be read later, perhaps.

I wondered if London had had a quiet night with no air raids or incendiary bombs. Maybe there would be a celebration, like eating the week's ration at one sitting—bacon with two eggs, an extra slice of toast, butter as well as marmalade, and endless cups of tea. The thought made me realize my thirst but I didn't feel like eating. As we doubled back along the road to collect our rucksacks, an idea crossed my mind. If there was a second phase this early, then there was plenty of time for a third phase, or even a fourth phase. With Dawson and Menday, I feared the worst. They would keep on bawling for action and I had a feeling that there was a lot more action to come.

After we had collected our rucksacks, dumped in the ditch on the road to Ouistreham, we started to march for the River Orne, our rendezvous with Lord Lovat. The sun shone. It was hot and we sweated under the weight on our backs, a column of hunchbacks, each better than the one at Notre Dame. It was a sight to break the steel mind of a Guards drill sergeant and drive him to tears.

Brigadier Lord "Shimi" Lovat had landed on the beach to lead the other commando units across the plain of Normandy. He ordered his piper, Millin, to play. The thin fluted notes of the piobh mohr floated high above the thunderous roar of guns and crump of high explosive. It was "Up wie the bonnets of bonnie Dundee" as the chief of the Frasers and his commando clan marched to the battle. It needed only the fierce Cameron pibroch, "Come ye sons of dogs and we will give you flesh", to herald another Montrose and a battle like Inverlochy—and no quarter asked.

Not that commandos would ask for quarter. They were aware of Hitler's order which read:

> I, therefore, command. From now on, German troops will destroy to the last man all enemy troops taking part in so-called commando raids in Europe or in Africa, whether it is apparently a case of soldiers in uniform, or of sabotage troops, with or without weapons, whether in battle or whilst escaping. It is immaterial whether they are brought into action by sea or parachute. Even should these creatures when discovered show readiness to surrender, they are on no account to be shown the slightest mercy. In each case a detailed report on this subject is to be rendered to the O.K.V. [German Supreme Command], for publication in the Wehrmacht Report.

At Dieppe, no quarter had been asked and no quarter had been given, when Lovat and No. 4 Commando had fallen to the German gun battery at Varengeville. Like highland hawks from the heather hillside, we had burned, reived and put to the sword, creating a funeral pyre of flame, smoke and destruction. Then we had returned to England.

This time there would be no going back. We were in Normandy to stay. The French civilians were now at great risk. We could never leave them or allow them to suffer the inevitable reprisals.

Bent under the load on my back, I plodded on, old Father Time with his scythe by my side. It wasn't him. It was Ronald Menday. He was giving orders.

"Donald, I want you to go forward as quickly as possible, contact brigade headquarters and find out the forming-up area for us. Get information and be ready for our arrival."

Good thinking, but not for me. I was to be an advance party of one. Me, with my hump, but I couldn't withdraw into my shell like a suffering snail.

A man nearby had a parachute bicycle. We had managed to bring a few of these light-weight machines ashore, just in case—and I was a case. My glance cabled my intentions and I saw the whiteness of his knuckles as he gripped the metal frame. I would need a jemmy to prize open the rigor mortis so I tried kindness. "I'll look after it for you."

He parted with the bicycle with all the reluctance of a good soldier under orders to use his lovely, lovely boots.

When I tried to mount, the weight of the full rucksack made me capsize but McCall came to the rescue. He began to haul the rucksack from my back and grunted, "Give me that. Me and Macaulay will see it gets there."

Macaulay, tall, curly-headed, the batman to Ronald Menday, grabbed one shoulder strap and McCall the other. They would carry it between them like a baby's portable cot.

Moments later, I was pedalling, knees rising and falling like the pistons of the *Waverley* steaming out of Largs. Unlike the skipper, I could not ring the telegraph for more power and there was no point in ringing for glory—not when you look like a bicycle-berserk chimpanzee.

The countryside was quiet, almost peaceful. The noise of battle receded, although I could hear the whisper of shells passing overhead. I was alone, everywhere was deserted—no people, no French, no British and no Germans.

I calculated it was roughly five miles to the bridge over the

Orne. Thick battle-dress cloth and the sun beaming down made me perspire.

Soon I was through the tiny hamlet of Bénouville and climbing the incline to the *mairie* at the crossroads. I raised my hand to salute a French couple who were standing, partly shielded by a stone wall which surrounded the village hall, the *mairie*, a solid masonry building. One day I would get to know them, Jean and Marie Deschamps.

Veering left and free-wheeling down the slope to the bridge over the River Orne, I braked to slow down, my eyes riveted on a glider parked on the far bank of the river. It was a fantastic piece of work. Major Howard of the 6th Airborne Division had landed his glider and crew, nose on to the bridge, with only inches to spare. He had managed to do it in the hours of darkness. He and his crew had nipped out smartly to surprise the Germans and to capture the bridge intact—an incredible feat of daring, a vital exploit.

This side of the bridge, I stopped. A lieutenant of the Airborne Forces greeted me. I told him that No. 4 Commando, like the Campbells at Lucknow, were coming, and my purpose was to contact No. 1 Special Service Brigade. He nodded and without speaking, half turned and indicated the bridge. My eyes followed in the direction he pointed. I hadn't noticed before. I did now.

Four crumpled shapes of soldiers in khaki lay strangely silent. I stared curiously, willing them to move. Slowly I turned back to the lieutenant. In clipped tones he answered my unspoken enquiry.

"Dead—German sniper up river in the trees somewhere—a sure shot—must be using a telescopic sight—we have people trying to flush him out—so far, no success."

Hobson's choice and I wasn't Hobson. I took time off to think but the thought process was disturbed as a jeep screeched to a halt. In the jeep were four paratroopers, wearing their own special type of helmet and camouflaged jacket. The driver, an officer, started a confab with the lieutenant. The other three looked me over unwinkingly—hard-eyed, hard nuts. Still, there would be no harm in asking.

My youth in Paisley had not been entirely mis-spent after all. Cycling with others of my own age, I had often hung on to the rear of lorries and vans to be transported at high speed, free of charge. It had been an exhilarating experience. Here was my chance to give a demonstration.

The officer driver agreed. The three hard nuts showed poker faces. The jeep backed up to get a flying start. The pilot revved the engine, let out the clutch and trod hard on the accelerator. Stones and dust smoked at the rear. I grasped a strut of the raised roof and the vehicle took off.

Careering down the slope it hit the surface of the bridge, bumping and jarring. Breathless seconds later we were over and protected by a line of trees in a road-cutting going uphill. Halfway up the slope the driver changed gear and slowed, giving me a quick glance over his shoulder. I let go and, just for the hell of it, did a little flutter with my hands, imitating a glider parting from its parent craft. The driver kept his eyes on the road, but I had success. The others grinned and gave me the thumbs-up sign.

At the top, the jeep disappeared, taking the right-hand fork. There, suddenly before me, out of the ground, appeared paratroopers. They were neatly entrenched and camouflaged. Surprised, I found myself looking down into the large mouths of rifles. Funny, they had never seemed so big before.

I shouted, "No. 4 Commando." They raised a cheer and pointed to the left fork on the road. I knew then I was cycling parallel to the river. The ground here was higher. I could see the puffs of white smoke mingling with the orange flash of big guns. They were still at it out there, at sea, pounding enemy positions far inland. The sun was shining, glinting and reflecting on rows of gliders parked in the right-hand field. A strange sight.

Over the huge field high poles had been staked out at regular intervals. I knew that the purpose of these was to stop gliders from landing, but in between the poles, and all over the area, glider after glider could be counted, all nicely parked, lined up as if ready for inspection. I wondered if some cheeky bugger of an airborne sergeant had insisted on dressing them by the right for my benefit.

The road here had a white powdered surface—probably crushed stone from the quarries at Caen. A white dust-storm was approaching me now. In it was Lord Lovat and his brigade major, Michael Dunning-White, was at the wheel of the jeep. They looked as if they were having a day out on the moors.

Before I could blurt out my report, they interrupted. How was I? How about Robert? And No. 4 Commando? Social graces first, the nasty horrid war we'll fix later.

On I went. I wasn't complaining but my "ass" was. Then I saw him, Derek Mills-Roberts, the colonel of No. 6 Commando. I had to report to him. I knew him. We all knew him.

He was a fearless lion with a bigger roar than Gaumont British. He carried a shillelagh, an Irish blackthorn. British Lions maul and put the boot in. Not for nothing was he known as "Mills Bomb Roberts". When he exploded, everyone felt the blast.

He gave orders and I listened. The brigade was collected around a crossroads. At a junior commanders' course at Scottish Command, they had told me to keep away from crossroads, the enemy might use these for ranging. They did.

A covey of screaming shells swooped down to explode and spray stones, earth and jagged metal. Mills-Roberts didn't even blink. I stood rooted to the spot.

Suddenly he stopped chewing his words and spitting them out of the side of his mouth at me. I shrank back as he roared, "Get these effing effers into effing cover, effing quick."

There was fast effing movement. The shelling ended, perhaps the Germans were petrified. That would be a fatal mistake. They should start moving, and not stop till they reached Berchtesgaden. Sooner or later, the colonel would have their guts for garters.

I turned away to meet the commando. They had bad news. They had doubled across the bridge over the Orne as fast as they could go but it hadn't been fast enough. The German sniper was still at large and he had aligned his telescopic sight and squeezed the trigger—Lieutenant Peter Mercer Wilson had been killed outright.

I paused to remember how F Troop had needed a fighting officer. They had got one and they could not have done better than Peter. He was ready to risk his life and on 6 June, he lost it.

Ronald Menday was shouting for me. In war, some don't get much time to remember, but then, some don't get much time to live. The war went on and No. 4 Commando went on. So did I—what else could I do?

Their calm before their storm. On board ship, 5 June 1944, Rifleman Keeley (*top right*) reads a thriller

Captains of No. 4 Commando troops. (*Left to right*) David Style, Bob Jennery, Peter Mercer Wilson, Mike Burness, Peter Beckett, Pat Porteous, VC, Jimmy James, Donald Gilchrist, Ken Wright, Len Coulson and David Haig-Thomas

(*Above left*) Philippe Keiffer, leader of the gallant French troops of No. 4 Commando. (*Above right*) Maurice Chauvet 'the wolf with a lock in his jaw', Premier Bataillon Marin Commando Français

Field Marshal Montgomery of Alamein with General 'Windy' Gale, 6th Airborne Division, at Ranville Cemetery, Normandy

Lovat, the MacShimidh, Chief of Clan Fraser, addressing his 'commando hawks' before they move off to the embarkation port

Shoal of ships involved in the D-Day operation

On reaching the Normandy coast, the commandos, some carrying bicycles, leave the LCTs and make for the shore

Troops move in to assault the German gun battery at Ouistreham

Sherman tanks help infantry to 'bash on regardless', Ouistreham

Hell and high water with explosives and live ammunition! Assault landing at Achnacarry

P.F.C Edward Trudell of 29th United States Rangers abseiling from the battlements of Achnacarry Castle

Farewell to Lieutenant-Colonel Charles E. Vaughan, commandant of the Commando Basic Training Centre, sometimes known as 'Rommel of the North'

Low tide at Flushing reveals a huge naval-type shell attached to an anti-landing stake lying at an angle

Dutch troops of No. 10 Inter-Allied Commando, at Flushing. (*Left to right*) L. Persoon, C. Van Gelderen, C. Van der Gender, J. Van Woerden, D. Van der Wal, C. De Ruiter, H. Van der Steen

H. M. Queen Elizabeth, the Queen Mother at the unveiling of the Commando Memorial at Spean Bridge, Lochaber, Scotland. With her are (*left to right*) Lord Lovat, Padre John Sutherland, General 'Lucky' Laycock and Mr Bill Gilmour-Smith

The Commando Memorial, the three bronze men on the hill above Spean Bridge

# 7
## Night Must Fall

Night must fall . . . and it did. But before darkness closed in on 6 June, the Germans started to probe, as if boxers, feinting, weaving and ducking, small groups reconnoitring, seeking to test us, trying to find out who, what and where we were. A tactical move before a counter-attack.

They found out. We were professionals, fit, tough, experienced and all carrying a hefty wallop. Perhaps they had hoped to catch us napping, punch-drunk, dazed and shattered after the onslaught of blows on the beaches. Commandos met them, toe to toe. The Germans were brushed off like the mosquitoes around the slit trenches dug in the defensive positions allotted to us.

No. 4 Commando had been given the honour of holding the extreme left flank of the British Army which rested on the sea. No. 3 Commando was on our right.

An honour won has to be held. Ronald Menday, now in command, had been given a difficult task. The defence of our particular area was full of problems for the countryside was close, hemmed by high hedges, tall earthy banks and heavily wooded. It was ideal for skirmishing with plenty of fields and little or no field of fire.

Our front position was long and troops were strung out in a thin line. There was no reserve apart from those we could muster at commando headquarters. We were assault troops who had never relished a sitting-duck role. It was an advantage that we had trained in Sussex and had carried out schemes in Brandon, Suffolk, on ground similar to that which we now occupied. Strange, too, that the town we had attacked on the beach, Ouistreham, was not unlike Troon in Scotland and Seaford in Sussex where we had been billeted. A training pattern had been created for the shape of things to come.

At Ouistreham there was a little harbour suitable for yachts and small craft. From there, the River Orne and the Caen Canal ran parallel all the way to Caen, the town famous for the castle of William the Conqueror and the two cathedrals, one for William and the other for his wife, Mathilde.

Headquarters took over the château at Hauger, a pleasant house with a cluster of farm buildings and cottages scattered around it. To one side, an orchard ran towards the sea.

At that Scottish Command course in Edinburgh, they had not only warned me about crossroads but also about buildings. If we thought they were suitable for us, so would our opponents. Any fool can make himself uncomfortable. The château was not chosen for comfort but for efficiency. Somebody had to operate the system, to issue orders, make reports, indent for rations, keep a tally of dead and wounded and those who were left to carry on.

What they did not tell me at that officer's course in Edinburgh was that wherever I went, Germans were going to seek me out and destroy me, and others with me. They had already killed David Haig-Thomas.

David, a lieutenant, had joined the unit at Winchester in Hampshire. At his first parade, we had been shocked as he appeared carrying his equipment over his arm as if a horse harness. We had hastily rushed to help him to get properly dressed before the adjutant, Michael Dunning-White, arrived. We were sure that Michael would suffer a heart attack.

Haig-Thomas was a tubby, round-faced, pink-complexioned, happy soldier. Acting as administrative officer on a tour of duty in the Faroe Islands, he had signed all indents for food and materials, "A. Hitler". He had got everything he wanted.

David had been at Cambridge. He had rowed three times for the university (a feat accomplished by only six men in all, of whom one had been his father) and then for Britain. While at Cambridge, he had written a book published under the title of *Leap before you Look*. His view was that if you dwelt too long, looking and thinking about problems and obstacles, you would never leap, never do anything.

Just before D-Day he had been sent off as liaison officer to the airborne forces. He was to be dropped with them, by parachute, on the night of 5–6 June. The "stick" went slightly astray and landed in a bog and swamp. To make up time, they set off hot foot to the r.v. (rendezvous). A German patrol ambushed the party and hurled stick grenades from behind a hedge and David, who was leading, fell to the ground. The others scrambled into a ditch. After a bit, a medical orderly crawled to where David lay. Although it was dark and the enemy were still about, he made an examination and found David to be dead. Ryder, David's diminutive batman, made it back to our lines to shock us with the news.

David Haig-Thomas had not thought twice to make his leap, a leap into darkness and occupied territory and to lead, as he had done in the Cambridge boat crew, but this time he had leapt into eternity.

We barely had time to enjoy our new surroundings before the Germans opened fire with artillery and mortars. A mortar bomb exploded on the gable-end of the château causing only slight damage. We had felt it and the roar was ear-splitting. No one needed a second bidding. Slit trenches had been speedily excavated.

I crawled out. I didn't fancy it much. It was a hole in the ground, an ominous 6 feet by 3 feet neatly measured to fit the body.

The builders, Messrs McCall and Maund had shown me round. They could have won an Oscar for their impersonation of estate agents.

Drained to one end, the trench had an empty tin fitted into one wall as a neat Hygena kitchen wall-cabinet. This would keep cigarettes and matches dry. Later some pin-ups would be added. A perfect home for this world and the next. Exactly to size, they would only have to fill it in and stick a cross on it.

They were grinning like happy apes. I grinned back, a satisfied customer who had gone to the right people. Thoughtfully, they had provided a roll-top sliding roof in the shape of a camouflaged green and brown waterproof gas cape. We carried these gas capes because they were lightweight and kept out water. We did not carry gas-masks bulging in canvas haversacks at the chest. We had enough to carry, laden like "pongos", the sure-footed donkeys used in the mountains of the North-West Frontier in India. These donkeys exude a nasty rippling "pong" at each step they take. Hence, "pongo", the rude name given to a soldier by the "medals on pyjamas" and "brylcreem boys" of the Navy and the R.A.F.

As evening drew in, the Germans continued their volcanic eruption of steel lava from guns, at regular intervals, dead on time, as if Big Ben chiming the hour at Westminster. If we went to sleep now, it would be forever.

A Russian called Tolstoy had written a book on *War and Peace*. It would not be a best-seller here, where peace was a thin flat shape and the size of an acid drop.

Who wanted to be out here digging his own grave exactly to size. Not me! I wanted to be back home in Paisley battling on the rugby field with Arnott Cochran, Dave McGhee, the Sims and the Pedens. Or serving cannon balls at tennis against Henry Dallachy, George Hill and Arthur McDowall. Better still, to be going through a tough assault course at Old Troon, St Andrews or Carnoustie, in jungle golfing adventures, where bunkers are soft sand, not concrete. There was no hope. Dawson and Menday did not play golf. It would do no good to mention it to Mills-Roberts. His shillelagh was a deterrent.

Somewhere in the theatre of Allied wartime operations, were two brothers, both commando leaders. One went into action with a bow and a quiverful of arrows, the other with a drawn sword. No one as yet had turned up with a blowpipe and poisoned darts. I kept quiet. There was no need to invite trouble.

Robert Dawson had arrived at Hauger with us. But we had at last convinced him that he must go back to have the wound in his head attended to. We did not want him dead, but alive. He would return to us. No one could lead us better, standing on a table, waving his arms and bawling out choruses of "*Alouette*".

Curled up in the slit trench I could hear the scream, plop and scrunch of H.E., high explosive. I cuddled the tommy-gun and whispered sweet nothings to it, like "Yes sir, you're my baby". Some baby! I had competition. Some other guy was singing to his rifle, "Night and day, you are the one" in a voice like a run-down gramophone.

At the chatter of machine-guns and the rattle of rifle fire, we stood to. That was easy. All we had to do was stand up, poke a tommy-gun or rifle over the trench top and align the sights. Those with rifles had bayonets fixed to form the spines of a porcupine, "*chevaux-de-frise*", iron spikes set in wood to repel cavalry. If Germans tried to jackboot in our defensive positions, they would have to be ironclads.

Our artillery had not started up yet. That was O.K. Supply lines from the beachhead would still be in the process of building up. We were here to protect them and give them time.

Meanwhile, the Germans could laugh and stop for a cup of tea while we pondered that he who laughs last, laughs longest. We had managed to squeeze in a few laughs already.

Slit trenches do not come with glossy "ads" specifying all "mod-cons". The occupiers have to get out from time to time for a variety of reasons, the wild desperate call of nature, for instance.

Field discipline is vital for health and sanitation. The toilets in the château were insufficient for all. Troops had dug a latrine, a long deep ditch, with a wooden trestle at each end and connected by a long carefully smoothed pole branch to form a perch.

As shelling started, commando roosters gave out high-pitched screams. Heads popped up out of trenches to see the pantomime. Battles and bombs were forgotten as comics sped out, bent double, holding up their trousers, flapping elbows as if wings, clucking and squawking, like hens outraged by a sadistic rapist cockerel.

"Disgusting! Mr Morris."

The regimental sergeant-major turned, startled, the laughter wiped from his face, as if a speck of dust from his immaculate equipment. Broad, burly shoulders, were squeezed out of his trench. The sparse hair on his nearly bald head lay flat avoiding my glance of approbation. We both did our best, but our best was none too good and we collapsed howling like hyenas. Sanity had returned.

In war there are many ways of dying. With No. 4, we could die laughing.

As explosions resounded we kept a check on each other, sometimes by calling out and at other times going round each trench. Was someone wounded, killed or buried alive?

Medical orderlies adapted jeeps to transport the wounded. They manufactured ambulances by hanging stretchers from the roof spars of these vehicles. These men, non-combatants, were not allowed the luxury of a slit trench. When duty called they were there, like the M.O., the medical officer, bandaging, tending and operating, offering up their own lives to save others.

As the battle raged, the thin lines of communication were often cut. The rubber-coated wire, the life-sinew of troops to headquarters, was broken time and again. Bombs or no bombs, it had to be repaired—and it was. The signal section under Captain Peter Beckett, a tall, dark, good-looking, lanky South African and his signals corporal, Ken Kennett, had no respite, maintaining R/T sets and telephonic contact, to create a network to the colonel at the centre.

When day broke, the heavens were blue and the sun shone on men in a warm sea of approval. Men stretching legs and arms, flexing muscles, tidying, cleaning weapons, shaving, washing and brewing tea. Tea. The beverage that beat a wee McEwans or a Tartan Special. Without it, Montgomery and the British Army would grind to a halt.

The sixth June had been a long, long day and the darkness of night had not been short. I eased myself out of the claustrophobia of the open trench grave.

An elbow dug into my ribs. McCall had a steaming hot mug of tea in one hand and two hard biscuits wedged in the other. I growled, "Where's the grapefruit, porridge, bacon and eggs, then?"

I caught the amused gleam in his eyes but it was too early for conversation. He turned away, elbows well out and went over to Maund, the C.O.'s runner. That pair were in cahoots. They were crooning over an old kettle and a battered pan. They had won these, of course. If they ever got to Paris, they would win the Eiffel Tower.

I sipped the scalding tea and dunked my biscuits. My teeth were good, but not a wolfhound's.

Some things would have to be done urgently. At the first opportunity, we buried our own dead. We chose the little orchard facing the sea and white cliffs of Dover. We held a short service paying our respects, simply, as soldiers do, with closest friends in attendance.

Sergeant Sellars of the Intelligence Section, an artist, would help me design a small memorial, a Celtic cross on top of a cairn of stones, one for each man of No. 4 Commando who landed on D-Day. An old Frenchman, a local stonemason, would cut the stone and erect the monument. He would inscribe on the cross the motto of combined operations "United We Conquer". Below, on a tablet, an epitaph would be written from Monty's Order of the Day.

> He either fears his fate too much,
> Or his deserts are small,
> Who dare not put it to the touch,
> To win or lose it all.

We had now a duty to see that they should not lose what they had gained—an everlasting peace.

Germans, too, were buried with care, with respect. No need to read out the Geneva Convention. Soldiers understand soldiers. Men who are disciplined seldom fail in their duty.

Dead animals had also to be buried. Some of these had died in the duck pond and there was risk of contamination. Mosquitoes were breeding in the stinking murky waters.

Shaving and washing was a problem. The water supply to the château had been damaged. Fires lit to boil water had to be screened so that smoke would not spiral up, like Red Indian signals giving away the position.

Some animals still lived. Sam Cooper and "Jacko" Jackson were staring intently at one now. Cooper had come to No. 4 Commando from the Royal Corps of Signals. Of medium height with sandy hair, Sam was a motor-cycle dispatch rider. He could claim to be the fastest and the best as he had competed in the T.T. races on the Isle of Man. Jacko was slim, loosely built and had black hair. He and Sam were married to girls in Troon, Ayrshire.

Leaning over the five-bar gate they eyed the animal as if farmers at the Royal Highland Show in Edinburgh, both calculating the weight and possible market demand. Sam spoke.

"Jacko! That's a pig."

Jacko's eyes widened. It certainly looked like a pig. It was pink, fat, snub-nosed and had four trotters. It was also grunting. There could be no doubt about it. So Jacko agreed.

"Y're right, Sam. That's a pig."

Sam scarcely heard him. With a far-away look in his eyes, he mused, "That pig reminds me of something, Jacko."

Jacko took time off to think. It was a long time since he had seen an animal like that. Not that it looked prehistoric, a dinosaur or a huge proboscidean quadruped. But the last three days had seemed like three thousand million years. There was no need to make a fool of himself so he answered cautiously.

"Yes, Sam. It reminds me of something too."

Suddenly Sam looked furtive. He squinted right and left and over both shoulders. There was nobody about. In a trice he vaulted the gate and drew his Colt automatic from the sheath holster hung from his waist belt. As a dispatch rider he was entitled to carry a Colt automatic. Colt automatics could be used for dispatching—and he wanted to dispatch something right now.

He fired twice in quick succession. There was no result. That was funny. Sam stared at the smoke escaping from the muzzle, then stared at the pig. Again he took aim, squeezed the trigger, and snarled, "Bloody pig!"

The pig, hit severely on its little pink tail, squealed horribly, leapt on all fours and turned, fixing its beady eyes on Sam, nostrils twitching, two muzzle openings aligned like a double-barrelled shot-gun.

Sam was not frightened of a pig, or anyone else, but he had his pride and showed it. He liked to be first in the T.T. races—he wanted to be first on this track.

As the pig took off to a flying start, Sam had already kicked for a starter and was screaming round the sty circuit intent on breaking every lap record, recklessly skidding on the muck and bouncing off the wall barriers. On the third lap, Sam was in trouble, with an air lock in the fuel supply and his brain box warning him of overheating in his manifold. And the pig was gaining.

Sam made it to the pits over the five-bar gate. He was covered in muck and the smell was not of oil. He had not won and had not lost. There was no official with a chequered flag. Only Jacko, bent double, tears welling in his eyes and holding both sides as if suffering from double appendicitis. But Sam did not laugh.

Sam came from Langold, near Ilkley, in Yorkshire. His father, a miner, had forced him to go into the pit. "Time you stopped playing about with motor bikes," he told Sam. When war came, Sam left the pit and joined the Royal Corps of Signals and later volunteered for special service, still sticking to his love of motor cycling.

Shortly after the pig incident, Cooper was wounded. With a small group he had watched a German pilot swoop past, aircraft engine screaming in protest. The aircraft suddenly swept upwards to do an Immelmann roll and then plummeted, diving towards the commandos now fingering their rifles. The whine from the leading edges of the plane was drowned as the aviator pressed the button to release a stream of machine-gun bullets. Sam and his little group of soldiers replied but Sam got a bullet through his ear.

Back in the château, a typewriter chattered staccato fashion. A bright-faced, fair-haired sergeant was operating it. A toilet roll was running under the roller like a ticker tape, not for stock exchange transactions, but for news. As runners came in, they could tear off at the perforations and return to their troops with the information. As Elliot said, "They can read all about it and the paper will come in handy."

Outside, in the courtyard, Pardo arrived with a message. I gaped at his steed, a thoroughbred, a magnificent horse. Pardo would know for he had been a stablehand. I watched him as he handled it, prancing and dancing, doing a little dressage. It was going to be tough on Pardo. I would have to tell him that the horse would have to be sent back to safety. It was not only valuable, it was vulnerable. Pardo took it well. He cared for his feet—but he cared more for the horse.

In a battle area, everything happens to everyone, everywhere at the same time. Each troop has its own fight, each man his own story. From the time that No. 4 Commando landed at dawn on 6 June, five days and nights would pass before they could claim sleep. The battle would rage, turned off and on like a bathroom tap—without the benefit of water to cleanse. A nightmare of garbled events, brought together by a catalyst to forge a united unit which would conquer. There were no nihilists, empty, believing in nothing. Each one believed in something, even if it was only himself! Seeing is believing—the good, bad and indifferent, the sad and happy, the fair and the ugly—and we were about to see a lot that needed believing!

## 8

# Whispering Death

The 15-inch guns of H.M.S. *Ramillies* swivelled silently as the warship cruised off the Normandy beaches. In the gun-turret the crew stood by, white flashproof monks' cowls covering their heads and shoulders. The huge guns projected missiles weighing just under a ton. When fired there would be the roar and flash of thunder and lightning.

Wearing ear muffs joined by a metal tiara, the radio operator listened intently for the crackling atmospheric message, a personal call from the F.O.B., fleet officer bombardment.

The F.O.B. was at F Troop position at Hauger, in a wood protected by a high wall and facing the Germans, who were some two hundred yards away forming up for an attack. High up, concealed in the leafy branches of a tree, he could observe as easily as a sailor in the crow's nest, with a bird's-eye view. Even better, he could act like a biased umpire sitting in the chair overlooking the front-line net on the centre court of the All England Tennis Club at Wimbledon. He would see that England served first, call out the range to mark the spot, then crisply command into the microphone, "Fire—shot one", which is the same as "Play—first service", only different.

As his call went over the air frequencies to the *Ramillies*, the radio operator, the signals officers, the gunnery officer and the gun crew, the troop waited by the wall, interested spectators hoping to see a big cannon-ball serve packed with a ton of high explosive.

It is a fact that these huge shells can be heard compressing the air as they sigh overhead. Len Coulson and Big Mac did not hear the sigh of "shot one". Neither did the troop. "Shot one" did not pass overhead.

A shattering explosion in the centre of their area caused a cascade of earth, stones and broken tree branches. Some trees were uprooted, falling dizzily, stripped clean of foliage. Stunned, shocked and incredulous commandos stared malevolently at the F.O.B. peering down, shame-faced, through greenery, while he gulped, "I'm terribly sorry chaps, but the next one will be over there!"

By the time he had got the range, the artillery forward observation officer of the 6th Airborne Division arrived to take over. This F.O.O. controlled the fire of 25-pounders. He laughed immoderately when told of the black mark his predecessor had chalked up. Len, Mac and the troop eyed him fatalistically and edged nearer to their slit trenches.

Almost as soon as the F.O.O. bawled orders into his R/T set there was a horrible whistling noise in the air above and the edge of the wood opposite was hidden by a series of eruptions giving off cloudy black smoke. The F.O.O. whooped in triumph while the troop look-out howled with glee and screamed like Oliver Twist, "Just the job. Give us some more."

Another salvo of twelve rounds rained down on the Germans and then the observation officer climbed down from his perch and said, sadly, "We're rationed to twenty-four rounds until we get some more ammo ashore. You've had your lot. So long!" As he went away the infuriated Germans replied with hate. Mortars and artillery boomed a crescendo of violence. With Teutonic cunning and precision they concentrated anti-aircraft guns on F and E Troops. Flak burst into the trees and splintered metal ricochetted down into the slit trenches. Men hastened to build protective roofs over the oblong holes in the ground, leaving only an opening to get in and out. Commando wolves snarled in their dens.

Except for one tall, brown-haired guardsman, Spearman. As look-out, he had to stay up a tree, tied to its branches by a toggle rope, five feet of thick strong hemp line with a loop at one end and a wooden toggle at the other. Linked by the toggle through the loop, the rope had many uses. Spearman was putting it to good use.

With all this flying metal, it was tough on him. But joined to the tree by the toggle rope, he knew that if he was wounded or even killed, he would not fall thirty feet to a broken back. He would hang up there, dead or alive.

Astonishingly, Spearman lived. Some didn't. Others were wounded. Captain Hutchison Burt, the wild, red-headed Scottish Leader of E Troop was seriously injured by a piece of shrapnel blasted down into his back.

Hutch turned his head to the small group attending to him. Frosty blue eyes dared them to do it wrong. Calmly, he asked, "Is it bad?"

"Pretty bad, sir!"

"Okay then, I'd better go back."

Hutch was taken to the regimental aid post and then sent back to hospital in England. He would not rejoin the commando, but he would stay in Special Service Group. He would be sent to the Holding Operational Commando at Wrexham, in Wales.

E Troop had now lost its captain, two subalterns and the sergeant-major. The troop was about a third of its normal strength and commanded by a section sergeant.

The worst was nearly over for the troops and it was nearly over for a pony. During the bombardment it had galloped into F Troop area to rear up on hind legs and whinny its cry for help. Ignoring the turmoil of noise and screeching metal, Sergeant McVeigh, a small tough Glaswegian, whose comments could be as skin-scorching as caustic soda, caught the pony and led it to his slit trench.

As McVeigh disappeared below ground the pony got down on all fours and stuck its head into the opening, like an ostrich, to be stroked and soothed as the sergeant told it lurid bedtime stories of the Gorbals, Hogmanay and the battles between Rangers and Celtic Football Clubs.

This happened each time the sentries blew whistles to warn that German artillery and mortars had opened fire. Odds were quoted. Who would get to the slit trench first, McVeigh or the pony?

Like the sergeant, the pony was a character and also a comic. When opportunity knocked, McVeigh, like others, had a quiet snooze in the open, under a blanket. The pony stole up, head down grazing delicately, rolling one eye to watch the sergeant. Gently with its teeth, it snatched the blanket off the sleeping warrior, then it was up and away, with the sergeant giving chase and yelling blue murder above the roar of the troop's laughter.

McVeigh fancied himself as a chef and had manufactured an oven from empty composite ration tins. He would cook a special dish—a succulent pie of Maconochie's stew with crumbly, crispy pastry on top made from crushed biscuits. His group's mouths watered. The delicacy would earn a *cordon bleu*.

When ready, McVeigh opened the oven and extracted the steaming ashet to cool. The aroma of culinary art pervaded the area. The sergeant was called away by his troop leader. Moments later he returned to serve his gastronomic feast but the ashet was empty.

There was the pony, pawing the ground, showing its teeth, nodding in approval, a gourmet's delighted saliva salute to the chef . . . encore! Encore! The whole troop collapsed suffering stitches as McVeigh screamed and shook his fists. This was horse-play all right.

C Troop was in the thick of it, positioned on the extreme left. Time and again the enemy tried to turn the position in a flanking movement. If they could get round C Troop, they would get behind us, perhaps even recapture the bridge over the River Orne and menace the beaches where vital supplies were being landed, the urgent stores of tanks, vehicles, food and ammunition.

We could not allow that. We wanted the bridge kept intact to allow our vehicles across the river, not German Panzers. But if we blew it up to deny it to the Germans, our supply problem would be made extremely difficult.

Then came the foul deed.

A white flag suddenly appeared in front of the troop position and a party of a dozen men ran forward. Mindful of the warning about the possibility of Poles wanting to desert to our side, David Style ordered the troop to hold their fire.

The flag party approached. When they were about fifteen paces away, David stood up with a man on either side of him to accept surrender. At once the flag party dropped flat. A German at the rear threw a stick grenade then loosed off with a Schmeisser sub-machine-gun.

The stick grenade burst near David shredding his leg and killing one of the men by his side. As David fell, he was caught in the chest and shoulder by a burst from a machine pistol, which also killed the man on his other side.

Hand to hand fighting followed. As fast as the Germans threw stick grenades, Sergeant-Major Peter King picked them up and threw them back.

A Troop too, had met the onslaught with their rifles, bayonets and their K for killer guns. In the ferment of fighting, there had been incidents aplenty—like the death of Sergeant Fraser.

A softly spoken Highlander from the Lovat Scouts, Fraser had not taken kindly to all the climbing done by commandos in training. He had no head for heights, the dizzy sickening vertigo on the precipices at Towyn in North Wales, where instructors did hand-stands high up at the edge of a perpendicular abyss. Only the persuasion of Lord Lovat himself had prevented Fraser from leaving the unit.

At Hauger, Fraser showed his true quality.

During a fierce German attack, he stood in the middle of a crossroads, coolly directing and encouraging his section in the face of murderous rifle and machine-gun fire. It was an incredible exhibition of bravery.

But this was something Fraser could understand, calmly pointing out targets as he would back at Beauly, in the north of Scotland, with a date at the butts and the grouse in the heather. This was different from those crazy cliff climbs.

The bullet and bayonet he understood. He was a fighting Fraser. Fighting like a Fraser—he died like a Fraser.

When finally he was cut down, his section fought like men inspired—as indeed they were—and the only Germans who weren't driven off were the dead and the dying.

There was the incident of O'Byrne, a wild Irishman in C Troop. A crack sniper, he had joined up with two other crack shots, one from No. 3 and one from No. 6 Commando. The three of them decided to go after the Germans as if on a field-outing to pot rabbits.

They came upon a German post. The Jerries were repairing their defences, but, by some strange chance, not one presented a target. The three deadshots speedily concocted a plan. O'Byrne sauntered out into the open and attracted the attention of the Germans by waving his hands and putting his fingers to his nose and calling them an interesting variety of names.

When the Germans leapt for their weapons to deal with the mad Irishman, the two hidden marksmen shot them with unerring aim. Then the three scampered off chuckling like schoolboys.

Knyvet Carr's mortar section had fired their mortars until the tubes were red hot. Obviously, he could not take up an O.P. to observe at each troop position. When direct radio and telephone communications failed, a relay system was set up via commando headquarters. It was not perfect, but it had some success. The system helped to keep the mortars firing and they did this in almost every direction as troop after troop requested support.

Vigorous and unflagging Knyvet came up with another idea. He put his section with their mortars onto jeeps, a tiny motorized column which raced up and down the road which ran parallel to our front. As soon as they had fired a few rounds from one position, they raced to another, misleading German calculations of the number of mortars ranged against them.

Ronald Menday decided to move his staff from the château to a battle headquarters. He chose a small farm building two hundred yards away in a leafy lane. There we established radio and telephone contact.

I shrugged off the dire warnings of infantry manuals on the subject of buildings. This tiny cottage could hardly be pinpointed on a map.

Some German gunner must have had good eyesight or good luck with a pin. A covey of shells fell from out of the blue. Shattering explosions sent bricks and rubble floating in the air. Ronald Menday was tossed, others thrown about.

Although there were no serious casualties, it was a blow. Those suffering shock threw it off. It was commonplace, an everyday occurrence. Telephone lines had gone, radio contact was almost nil. We badly needed a reserve to help stop the gaps and to hit back. Ronald Menday sent me to No. 3 Commando urgently.

McCall and I set off at the double through the wood. We were challenged and passed through to a clearing. McCall crowded up on me and together we stood and gaped.

At the edge of the clearing, an awning had been built. Underneath sat Peter Young, the colonel of No. 3 Commando, wearing an Arab head-dress. Members of his staff were grouped round him as if in attendance on one of the Pharaohs. He beckoned me and I went forward, unsure whether to stand to attention and salute, or to fall down, grovel and kiss his hand.

He agreed to move one of his troops and take over our E Troop position. This was just what we wanted. We would have a mobile force to strike where needed.

Meanwhile, back to headquarters, Pat Porteous of D Troop had called for assistance. Pat had won the V.C. at Dieppe and he was doing his best to get another. Ronald Menday grabbed Jimmy James, the Welshman, and James with all headquarters staff went into action. It had been swift and furious and the Germans had been routed. The encounter left D Troop with two officers, a sergeant-major and twelve men. Elliot, Beacall, Marsden and Bagnell were now smirking, cleaning and handling their rifles the way Dad tenderly baths the new baby. Before life became impossible I reminded them, "You'll get no promotion this side of the ocean, so cheer up me lads, bless 'em all."

I checked my watch. It was time I went out. Rocket-firing Beaufighters were expected to put in a strike. The aircraft would pass over us, hedge-hopping. They were known as the "Whispering Death".

We saw them a second before they whispered past. We stuffed a finger in each ear and felt the tremor of the air thrust. Then we heard the deep "whoosh" like a drawn-out sigh, as missiles were expectorated, trailing vapour, feathering their way to the target. A succession of thumps followed, while the aircraft climbed steeply, banking and cavorting to avoid the anti-aircraft barrage of shrapnel. Moments later they returned waggling their wings. We looked up and waved our green berets.

For training, some of us had gone up in aircraft like those. Lovat had arranged it. The pilots had eyed our green berets and given us broad smiles. When we returned to earth, our legs had been drained of sap. Flying officers and flight-sergeants had softened us up then, but not half as much as they were softening up the Germans now.

Saturday, 10 June, saw a grand finale in which all the orchestra took part, their instruments of war resounding and echoing in the open-air theatre. It had been a five-day continuous night and day performance tuned to highly strung concert pitch. There could be repeat shows later in the provinces. Almost certainly we would go on tour.

We had almost forgotten how to sleep. The longer we stayed awake, the less we needed sleep. In the lull of battle, sentries stood fast, others relaxed, red-eyed, letting exhaustion pour through their veins, stretching luxuriously, dropping off on the spot, to sleep as blissful as the dead.

Of the 430 British officers and other ranks who landed on D-Day, there were 160 left, while but 70 of the French remained of their 200.

When I awoke, it was Sunday. I yawned, stretched and prised open hooded eyelids gummed drowsily tight. I peered at the sunshine and the hive of activity—men shaving, washing, brewing tea and cleaning weapons. Despite the stinking pond, mosquitoes and poor supply of water, they managed to keep clean and tidy. I followed their example.

Sunday is the day of rest, a day to go to church, to pray for the love of God and mankind. There are different kinds of men, some showing love and others exuding hate. So far I had seen a lot of hate, but then I had also witnessed a lot of love. Foul deeds going hand in hand with tiny actions by men, shining bright.

Here men lived, loved, laughed and died. They loved women, children, animals and their companions. They were not beasts of the jungle. There were few, if any, hard-eyed killers. They were specially trained, tough, facing up to hardship and danger. Their fury was that of men stung into maddened battle fervour so that, come what may, they would succeed in their purpose.

We could not expect to go to a church parade, all beezed up. It would be nigh impossible for the brigade padre to get round all the troops scattered on the ground like chaff. F Troop held their own Sunday service, standing in the slit trenches. With only head and shoulders above ground they listened to Len Coulson, their troop leader, read the lesson, and silently bowed their heads to hear the words of prayer, with the faith of Covenanters.

My own regiment was The Cameronians (Scottish Rifles). McCall had admired my silver badge with the Douglas star, lovers' knot and garland of Scottish thistles. I had given him one and he wore it proudly. As Covenanters, each officer and man was issued with a tiny copy of the New Testament. It was part of a man's kit and had to be shown at inspections. I carried mine always. Cameronians were allowed to take their rifles into church, having first posted sentries at each corner of the building. If the service was held in the open, we went armed and look-outs were posted at vantage points on the hills. It followed tradition. Supporters of Cameron had been surprised at church service. The doors had been locked and barred from the outside and then the building had been set on fire—it had been a living cremation.

Here, at Hauger, in Normandy, in the year 1944, sentries were posted and men listened to the gospel, fingers on the trigger.

A soldier was sitting cross-legged, cradling his rifle and using the pull-through. Deftly, he dropped the brass weight, caught it, tugged smoothly on the cord and the oiled rag flipped out to be neatly held. He peered up into the barrel. He was satisfied. He offered it to me for inspection but I waved it away and squatted beside him.

He took a cigarette and I lit it and then lit one for my myself. We blew smoke like flak and the mosquitoes buzzed off. Cigarettes as well as other things were in short supply but the Americans had been generous. They had given cartons of the weed to the 6th Airborne Division and they had shared the wind-fall. That was what it was all about—sharing.

He was using his oily rag to polish the stock of his rifle. Maybe he was saving it for an antique. In time, he would speak. He spoke.

"Have you noticed anything peculiar about this place, sir? I have been wondering about it for days. I've only just found out what it is."

That made me think, starting off the memory bank. Colonels who sang "*Alouette*", waved shillelaghs, brandished swords, ran about with bows and arrows, and acted like Genghis Khan. Troops with hot pies and ponies, listening to the Bible stories told by a guy who had a nose like a professional bruiser. There was lousy water, Maconochie's stew and dog biscuits. People were firing shells, mortar bombs, and shooting with live ammunition. Toilet rolls were used in typewriters. No street of a thousand delights, no Glenfiddich either, and worse, no in, out, or pending baskets, and I went on to complete a dozen sheets of foolscap, both sides.

I answered carefully.

"No, I hadn't noticed anything peculiar."

He paused in his life's work to tell me. "No birds."

What did he expect? The key to the local harem. This wasn't Cairo. We were living like monks in an open-air monastery without a garden. There wasn't even the swagger of a kilt. The song went "A Gordon for me, A Gordon for me, if you're no a Gordon, ye're nae use tae me". He didn't look kinky. He proved it. Reading my mind, he added, "The feathered kind".

He was right. I felt the silence. I heard the silence. It was the end of the world. No twittering, no fluttering of wings. War had desecrated this place and made it desolate. Wildlife had flown away or gone to ground. A soldier, with a licence to kill, had made his observation, his simple protest.

At night, patrols were sent out to sweep no-man's-land. The French had discovered a store of wine at the farm in the Bois de Bavent. The Germans knew about it too. The French set traps and got the wine, and the Germans as well.

Derek Mills-Roberts went out on patrol by himself, using a throat microphone and gave commentaries emulating Alvar Liddell on the B.B.C., London calling. We speculated among ourselves on what might happen if the Germans met Mills-Roberts. We shuddered at the prospect of the Germans, standing to attention, while the Brigadier told them who he was and what they were, in language well interspersed with four-letter words.

Mills-Roberts was now the Brigadier of No. 1 Special Service Brigade. We had been stunned when Lord Lovat had been gravely wounded. We were used to his tall debonair figure striding with us. He had led at Lofoten, Boulogne, Dieppe and the D-Day landings, with the flair of Montrose, leading and encouraging. We had followed. Example is inspiration and No. 4 Commando and No. 1 Special Service Brigade had been inspired.

We were inspired again by Brigadier Derek Mills-Roberts of the Irish Guards. When he roared like a lion, the animals of this wartime jungle would tremble and run.

# 9
## Women with Something to Live For

My watch agreed with my belly. It was lunchtime and I had a date with the French.

Philippe Keiffer greeted me with the air of the manager of Maxims welcoming an honoured patron. Others subjected me to bear hugs. I gasped and counted broken ribs.

They escorted me to the table and I gaped at the arrangements. An oblong pit had been excavated big enough to hide a Crusader tank. Over the deep cavity hung a camouflaged awning of waterproofed sheets interlaced with foliage. Underneath, a rudely made table was flanked by rough wooden benches.

Dazed, I sat down. Waiters hovered and proffered wine. Nearby I spotted a home-made enclosure in which a young calf was tethered and chickens strutted and pecked at the ground. The French enjoy eating. They made sure that they would.

Soup, veal, vegetables, followed by Camembert cheese washed down with wine and large mugs of tea. In the babble of gesticulating conversation and laughter, I waved my arms, shrugged, spread my hands rapturously.

"*Mais oui, Philippe. Votre cuisine est magnifique.*"

This won applause, the chef and waiters joining in the hand-clapping. I told myself that I had nothing to worry about, it was only the Germans at the other side of the field. So why not eat, drink and be merry—tomorrow might never come. It was as safe as the Bank of England. I worry about these things and I wondered, with the sort of friends I had, was the Bank of England really safe?

Returned to the fold, uncaring of things that creep and crawl and go bump in the day as well as by night, I took time off to sit by my slit trench. A whole long minute to contemplate, aping a Greek philosopher, philosophizing.

Captain Len Coulson wore the badge of the Durham Light Infantry. He boasted that his regiment held the long standing record of the 1914 war when his regiment had been in the front line for 51 days. No. 4 Commando would exceed that. They would be the forward troops in action for 83 days.

Disturbed in my mental search for wisdom, I looked up. McCall was there, smiling broadly. It seemed that nothing was impos-

sible in this world because, balanced on four fingers and clipped
securely by a thumb on top, he held three slices of bread. I barked,
"Where the hell did you get that?"

"The administrative officer—Cap'n Cross, sir."

"So?"

"Cap'n Cross, he was down at the beach getting rations and met
the lads from the *Astrid*."

McCall was doing well. He needed encouragement. I gave it.

"Uhuh?"

"The lads from the *Astrid* asked Cap'n Cross if we, us, No. 4
Commando, needed anything. Cap'n Cross did a big think, then
said, 'Bread'. The Navy lads said, 'Bread?' Cap'n Cross, he said,
'Yes, bread'. So the Navy lads jumped into their boat and went
back to the *Astrid* and the whole ship's crew gave up their ration—
a slice and a half for every man of No. 4 Commando."

Jock looked exhausted, it was a long spiel for him. I watched
him split one of the slices and give me my share. Since landing,
we had fed on Maconochie's stew and hard biscuits. If we ate
much more biscuit, we would soon be wagging our tails and
giving a paw. The French had fixed their own cuisine and had
their own private farmyard and wine cellar. The best we had been
able to do was to collect a few bottles of wine, which had gone
on a little battlefield party in aid of *entente cordiale*.

I licked my lips. Bread. Real honest to goodness bread. White
soft fluffiness yielding to finger-tip touch and compactly held
together by a dainty light brown crusty strip neatly rounded at the
corners—manna from heaven!

Slowly, gently, my teeth bit right through, I chewed delicately,
digesting every morsel of the succulent savoury moulded by the
*Astrid*'s chef. With my tongue, I sought out each minute scrap
misguided into a tooth crevice. I licked my fingers, sighed, looked
down at my battle dress and the ground below. Not a particle had
escaped.

Our eyes met. I raised my mug and Jock raised his. I
murmured, "Here's to Cap'n Cross, the Navy, the *Astrid*, and all
the ship's company."

The deafening tortured scream of the jeep's brakes made me
lurch to one side. Almost before it jolted to a halt, Lofi was out
and I was using unarmed combat to fight off his embrace. I had
only one spine and the army had kept it straight.

Lofi was burly and barrel-chested. With his dark hair, flashing black eyes and bull-like strength, he had the temperament of a pirate. He was waving his arms and talking quickly.

"Donald, 'ow would you like to 'ave the bath, in clean water, at a château—and afterwards, perhaps, some wine with the chatelaine?"

A bath in clean water? At Hauger it was difficult enough to get water to shave and get a sponge down. The duck pond was stinking. Mosquitoes were breeding in murky pools and in long swamp-like grasses. The French had cornered the wine market at the Bois de Bavent. They had ousted the Germans to get it, so that was fair. I fancied the idea of a château, especially with a resident chatelaine. Lofi was the fly in the ointment; with his flair for playing D'Artagnan, I would be acting second musket.

It was not far to the château of Bénouville, but far enough for discomfort. With Lofi driving, foot hard down on the pedal, gesticulating with both hands and talking, I was bounced round the jeep seat cushions like a snooker ball seeking the safety of a hammock pocket.

We slithered to a stop in front of two huge stone pillars on which hung heavy, wrought-iron gates pulled back. Beyond lay an overgrown leafy drive-way, showing guiding ruts through the weeds.

I struggled with my pulse rate. Lofi was speaking, his hands waving in front of my face.

"Donald, I forgot to tell you. It is not now the château, it is, 'ow do you call it *en Angleterre*? Ah yes, it is now the 'ome for the unmarried mothers."

Thunderstruck, I was the tree stripped of its bark, dead wood being transported at high speed up the tree-lined path in park land to scrunch on the gravel in front of a huge mansion. Solid rounded stone pillars rose up from the slabs to the portico. A gracious house about the size of Belleisle House in Ayr. The jeep seemed out of place. The château merited a carriage and six white horses.

The woman who greeted us was not old, nor was she young. Her black hair was drawn back but not severely. Brown eyes twinkled behind hornrimmed spectacles. She was dressed in black, had a curvacious figure and wore neat black shoes ornamented by metal buckles. I could tell she was French—and a woman.

Lofi was quick. Already he was bending over her hand oozing

charm and audacity. Who did he think he was? The Count of Monte Cristo? To hell with Lofi, it was my turn. I swept off my green beret, took her hand and bent low, making a leg. I smiled— a slinky, sneaky, sexy smile and murmured, "*Enchanté, Madame, vous êtes ravissante.*"

Lofi was coughing up his guts but I had scored. Her eyes sparkled. She was pleased with the performance.

We had baths, in clean water, and afterwards, we sat in the comfort of the château, drinking wine with the chatelaine, Madame Vion. Then she showed us round her domain.

All the huge rooms had been split into cubicles, each containing a bed and a cot, with all the other articles necessary for a mother and newborn child. The mothers had the benefit of each other's company and they could walk in the estate and share their problems. Whether the children were born of French, English or German fathers mattered not to Madame. The mothers and children were as much in need of love and affection as any other mother and child. At the château of Bénouville, there was, for them, love, affection and protection.

When the Germans had arrived they had wanted the château for their headquarters. Then they had desired it for a hospital for soldiers recuperating from wounds and the ordeal of the Russian Front. Lastly, they had required it for a strong-point, dominating the distant beaches. To all their demands, commands, pleas and entreaties, Madame said, "No".

The Germans gave dire warnings of what might happen to her and her charges if Allied landings took place in Normandy. Madame remained cool, calm, collected and adamant. So far, the good God had protected her and all in the château. She would continue to put her trust in Him.

The German High Command had had to retreat, in nail-biting, frustrated fury, before a woman. A woman with something to live for.

Men, I supposed, needed something to die for—a challenge to their masculinity perhaps. If that was what men wanted, this was the place and now was the time.

Mortaring was the bane of our existence. At every mealtime, almost without fail, a bomb would whine over and crash down somewhere in the unit area. Sometimes a single bomb, sometimes a concentration over a period of two hours, ruining food and splattering those around the petrol cooker, above the roar of which the noise of the descending bomb could not be heard.

Night-time was the favourite. When the sun went down mosquitoes would make it impossible to sleep. Then as darkness fell, the guns started to fire in the distance. Dark shadows of sentries listened unseen while frogs in a stagnant pool began their croaking evensong.

Fighting patrols slipped quietly out from the troop lines to bait traps and dominate no-man's-land. Animal instinct brought success with survival, and survival meant that you could do it all again tomorrow.

Sentries stayed alert to forestall small groups of Germans carrying explosive charges. They attempted to get through our lines and cause havoc, their main target being the bridge over the Orne.

Panzers had been heard but by some fate had been directed towards Troarn. An S.P. (self-propelled) gun on a tracked vehicle, prowled behind the enemy lines. Every now and then it fired a shot, then it could be heard grumbling as it moved to another position. One of these days we would fix it. It was only a matter of plotting the halting place of that gun and our artillery would hand out curtains, free, without coupons.

We detested the 88-mm S.P. guns which fired a high-velocity shell, the speed of which gave no warning, although it did little damage to those under cover, except to their taut nerves.

For me, the weeks till the end of June would be rolled into one. Events would happen. I didn't know. I was living in the present not in the future.

The Colonel was back, his head wound healed. He had returned to take over command from Ronald Menday. He was sitting at the wheel of a jeep, and he was waiting for me. The tank battle for Caen was about to begin. He wanted to see it.

While he drove he told me that the Germans at Salenelles had surrendered.

Salenelles was on the opposite side of the River Orne from that on which we landed. The Germans had made the position into a strong-point. We had been informed about it. The walls were as thick as the pyramids and had big guns facing the sea. The guns could not be traversed to fire to a flank or inland.

Since our landing, the German defenders of Salenelles had held their peace. We had sniffed around the site but had been ordered to bypass it and not waste men, time or ammunition. This proved to be good thinking. The Germans had now come out with their hands up.

In my mind something stirred and I thought of Mademoiselle Pigache, a retired schoolmistress. Her black hair, severely brushed, showed strands of white. Grey-blue eyes were darkly encircled, accentuating the pallor of her face. She suffered from migraine. One foot was slightly deformed, the result of an accident when a child. Normally she wore white sand shoes in direct contrast to her preference for a black dress, as hard shoes caused her pain. Only on special days or at church did she wear shoes, low-heeled, black suede. Her English was surprisingly good. She surprised me.

"I have a secret which I have told to no one. I have kept my secret for a long time but I want to tell it to you now."

For a fraction of a second she paused to gather her thoughts. What secret could this delightful woman hold? The ravages of war could take people into dark corners, mind-bending crises, nerve-screeching decisions, foul revolting deeds. It could not be that. Then perhaps a tale of romance, of wartime, heart-breaking unrequited love?

"It was some time before the invasion. I went to Ouistreham to buy some things. Going into a shop I collided with a very tall, immaculately dressed German officer. He apologized as he bent to help me pick up parcels I had dropped. Suddenly, he seemed embarrassed and there was a moment of confusion, parcels being thrust into my hands. Very quickly he saluted, clicked his heels and strode off. Inside the shop I tried to collect my wits. The German officer had seemed upset, almost distressed. I wondered about that since there seemed to be no reason for his anxiety. It worried me, until all at once I knew—he had apologized in English.

"Abruptly, I paid for my purchases and hurried out to the pavement, but he was nowhere to be seen. I walked back to my house very slowly and told myself that I was a very silly old woman, day-dreaming. Perhaps it was something I wanted to happen. You know, an old schoolmistress and a tall, handsome British Secret Service Agent. By the time I had reached my villa I had convinced myself, and forgot all about the matter.

"Then something happened that was very strange. It was a few months before the commandos came. There was much excitement here and at Salenelles where the Germans were. They had built a fortress there with much concrete. There was now much polishing and cleaning. High-ranking German officers came to inspect Salenelles. They came in an open car. There was marching and saluting. Then they went away and life became normal again."

She hesitated. The unsmoked cigarette was burning my fingers. I stubbed it out, as I thought. An inspection was normal. We did that sort of thing too. As if reading my mind, she spoke.

"Except that, about a week later, the same thing happened again. The Germans at Salenelles were surprised and suspicious. The second lot of high-ranking German officers were locked-up. You can imagine the alarm, the telephoning, the questioning, the interrogating. After, the activity was intense. The second lot of German officers were found to be genuine.

"Now then," she exclaimed, "I want you to tell me something. If the second lot of high-ranking German officers were genuine— who, then, were the others? Maybe I wasn't dreaming after all. Maybe that German who bumped into me in Ouistreham did apologize in English. Perhaps I am not so old and silly. It has been my secret. It has worried me. Now that I have told it to you, I am content."

Madelaine Pigache had been a schoolmistress. She was used to adding up, assessing fact, putting logic to reason. In war, stories and rumours abound. But I held a tiny piece of the jigsaw puzzle. It might fit and complete the picture.

I took my time and marshalled the facts. Aerial photographs gave a great amount of information. From these photographs, it was possible to measure mathematically the circumference of gun pits, strong-points and the depth, breadth and length of anti-tank ditches.

On the Dieppe raid, Jimmy McKay, the Royal Engineer officer, had carried explosive charges ready made to fit the breeches of the guns. After the charges had been blown, Krupps would be in tears. They would be unable to effect repairs. But how had it been possible to gauge the calibre of the guns? By using an instrument, aerial photographs could be viewed in three dimensions. But could this read the maker's name and specification of the guns?

No. 4 Commando had been informed of the German strong-point at Salenelles. We had been ordered to bypass the site. I had studied enlarged aerial photographs. Perhaps scientific boffins had their equations to calculate intricate details. I was sceptical of calculated guesses.

I told Mademoiselle Pigache. "The secret of Salenelles remains a mystery to me. Perhaps some day I shall find out. I cannot, for certain, confirm your story. You have kept your secret at a time when one word from you could have cost the life of a British Agent. "And", I added, "Just remember, many odd things happen during a war. You must know, as I do—fact is often stranger than fiction!"

For the first time, I noticed the speed of the vehicle. He was driving the "hosses" and covered wagon like an old-timer going way out west. When he trod on the brake, I jumped out, Wyatt Earp, ready to thumb the hammer of the Colt automatic. Breville was deserted, no saloon, no baddies.

Robert was off and going up the tall bank. I scrambled after him on hands and knees, to lie at his side, focussing binoculars to sweep and scan the plain below. From here we had a panoramic view, a wide screen, a three-dimensional picture—in colour.

The armoured division was rolling, pennants flying, their tracked vehicles spurning the ground. The cavalry were charging for Caen, guns spitting flame and smoke. Soon they would be close in and the fighting would be hand to hand, parry and thrust.

Rising dust filled the air with the bitterly pungent smell of oil and burnt cordite. Enemy shells fell from the heavens to explode. throwing up great geysers of earth and metal. Pride chewed at my guts and welled at my throat. Down there, gallantry was burnished, untarnished, shining armour-bright.

Monty had made it clear to us. When the battle was joined it would be "nae bother at a' ". The hinge of the door was at Caen. He intended to slam it in the face of the Germans, using his famous right hook.

The tank crews sweating it out in the ring would not be following Queensberry rules. This was not going to be a polite punch on the nose. It was going to be a helluva big kick in the crotch. The scene was indescribable, awesome, an epic no Hollywood producer could ever equal.

Robert moved first. He jerked his head. "We'd better get back. Anything could happen now."

I went along with that. I went along with him. It happened all the time.

Philippe Keiffer and Alex Lofi were standing waiting for us. Excitedly, they started gabbling in French.

I would have to do something about this language. When we got to Paris to leer at long-legged gorgeous women, to eat oysters, caviare and drink champagne, I didn't want to be left outside the Bal Tabarin, with a poke of fish and chips and a bottle of Burdock stout. I had been thinking up slinky ideas for French women's liberation.

Keiffer and Lofi climbed aboard. We were going to the out-skirts of Caen. With Ripley, I could believe it or not. With this bunch I could believe anything.

Members of the Resistance movement, the Free French Forces of the Interior, were ready to meet us. In Normandy, they were known as the "Scameroni" from the name of one of their leaders, a Corsican, who had been caught and tortured by the Gestapo, but had remained silent. As witness to his courage and fortitude, the group had continued operations.

Inside the room there was an air of jubilation. The Scameroni had played a lone, isolated, desperate game of cat and mouse, with the Gestapo. The Scameroni did not look like mice.

The leader of the group, Leonard Gille had dark wavy hair, black eyes, and an aquiline face with a devil's dimple at the point of his chin. He was charming enough, but those black eyes had a glitter. There was a blonde, probably about thirty, with a pink and white complexion. She was slim, with blue eyes and seemed quiet compared with the others.

But it was to the only other woman in the room that my eyes were drawn as if by a magnet. Vivacious brown eyes flecked with gold were set in a round, nicely modelled face and her head topped with glorious tawny hair. She was irresistibly attractive. A young lioness—Janie.

Her recent exploits had been during the bombing and shelling of Caen. She had mingled with the refugees, caught up in the focal point and desperately seeking a temporary haven. Janie had disguised herself as a filthy dirty old woman, with unkempt hair, dressed in rags and wheeling a dilapidated pram, heaped with the flotsam and jetsam of war. The odd assortment of rubbish con-cealed a transmitter. By this means, she had been able to pass back information about the flow of homeless and the movement of enemy troops. She had been detained by the Germans for ques-tioning. Allied aircraft had swept down strafing and harassing. In the confusion, she had slipped away to carry on her mission.

Earlier, she had been sent out to bring in an R.A.F. pilot who had been shot down. He had landed safely and had hidden his parachute. Now he had to place his life in the hands of a woman. Janie led him by devious routes towards the town. It was hot and tiring, with nervous tension building up from keeping constantly alert. At the outskirts of Caen, she decided they must rest and await the cover of darkness.

They made for a nearby farm with its tangle of buildings. Here they might find a suitable hidey-hole for two people. For some time they observed, then decided to chance their luck, stealthily creeping and crawling to the barn, to lie breathing sighs of relief.

The sounds were faint at first, but gradually increased. Soon they heard the whine of vehicle engines and the staccato bark of motor cycles approaching. In horror they listened to the din in the farmyard, interspersed with guttural shouts and commands. They had little time to spare so they jumped up and dived into the hay piled at one end of the barn, to burrow deep and cower in silence.

It was not a moment too soon. Jackboots clattered on paving slabs and pounded the earthen floor as German soldiers entered, their voices loud and harsh. Equipment jangling and scraping and the scuffing of the ground made Janie's blood run cold. The Germans were here to stay.

Suddenly, there was a new menacing sound. The tramp of boots ticked off seconds and pulse beats as they came closer, closer and closer. Abruptly they stopped. Janie held her breath and listened to the thump of her heart in an interminable fraction of a lifetime.

Then it happened. Something came driving down into the hay to jar and twang in a curious tuneless echo. The echo struck a chord, and she knew—the German was violently thrusting the prongs of a pitch-fork into the hay. Again, and it was closer, while she heard a voice, almost drowned in raucous guffaws of laughter.

"What do you expect to find, Hermann? A little French mouse?"

The fork drove in again and again. This German soldier was thorough. One more time, thought Janie, and I shall be dead. It was near enough. She cringed, shut her eyes, and prayed.

Derisive yells from the other Germans took effect. Janie heard his curse and the clatter of the implement as he threw it to one side. Her prayers had been answered. Then there was the incredible, ear-splitting noise of aircraft, pilots boosting the Rolls-Royce Merlins to a tumult, and the lung-bursting, blood-sucking vent of spleen, the explosion, crashing, and ricochet of high-velocity cannon shells which brought fear and weakness into the bowels. This was no place to rest and certainly no place for German soldiers. With cries, commands, curses, cranking of engines and the spluttering of motor cycles, the German motorized columns went off, faster than they had come.

Like a Royal Canadian Mounty, Janie got her man and brought him in.

At Caen the Resistance group at this time existed by moving from one hide-out to another and, at that moment, were in the cellars under the rubble of a bombed-out building.

The R.A.F. officer had got his second wind. He eyed his French saviours. He saw that they were unshaven, scruffily dressed, and none too clean. H'm! No *esprit de corps*. He'd show 'em. He started to clean his flying boots, brush off the dust and stains on his uniform and return to his impeccable, suave, debonair self. If he had to do or die, he would do so properly dressed, spick and span, like a decent chap, an Englishman and a gentleman.

He insisted on shaving every morning. Of course, he could not know that his rescuers had to risk their lives each time they needed water to drink, let alone shave and wash. His demand for shaving water caused an uproar. The Frenchmen threw up their hands in despair and complained sourly in anger. It had been difficult for Janie to soothe them.

Afterwards, she scolded them. This R.A.F. officer fought for them and risked his life for France. He was one of them, he was their honoured guest. Shaving water he must have, she insisted.

The Frenchmen grumbled, but the R.A.F. pilot was supplied with water to shave each day. He would not be told until after the war the risk and danger involved.

"Men!" Janie shrugged her shoulders despairingly. "Men!" She repeated, "Zey are not onlee stupid—zey are imposseeble!"

What with the wine and the knowledge that there were still some women left in the world, I needed some shut-eye by the time I was dumped from the jeep beside my own little slit trench at Hauger. But would I get it?

Shelling and mortaring were now spasmodic. Certainly, I had less to worry about. My rucksack and extra kit had been blown to bits when H.Q. had been hit. I had only what I stood up in. They say that he who travels lightest, travels fastest and farthest. Berlin would suit or Paris even better.

At least, since D-plus-one, we had been spared the attentions of the Luftwaffe. On the evening of that day, a lone German flyer had zoomed across the tree-tops towards the Orne, machine-gunning everything in sight. He had returned a few minutes later, sweeping over us, to return into his own territory.

Later, planes had droned overhead and we had watched the tracer of ack-ack curve slowly up. Within seconds every gun in the vicinity was brought into action. The sky was criss-crossed by coloured streaks, graceful constellations of glowing red spheres bursting into myriads of satellites. Above the deep bark of guns we could hear the whine of falling bombs and the rumble as they burst and exploded. It was a wonder that any aircraft could slip through that interlocking pattern of fire and light, an aerial blitz.

One plane did not. There was a sudden orange flash, a magnesium snap of brilliant hue and a ball of fire cometed its course to earth. Minutes later another followed it to make a second bonfire.

Shortly afterwards, dive-bombers filled the night with shrill horror as their pilots tortured aircraft engines and aerial struts into a terrifying, screaming, nightmare plunge. They had not waited long, but long enough to merit a string of terrible curses from those of us below.

They had not come back. But we still had to thole the artillery. Both sides took it in turn to keep us awake. I got my head down. These damned gunners had a perverted sense of humour. I needed some "shut-eye". There were no sheep around here so I began to count shells. I got to seven . . .

If you are tired enough, you'll sleep. I had slept and feeling refreshed, was ready for anything. I stretched, yawned and blinked.

Philippe Keiffer was in earnest conversation with the Colonel. Robert crooked a finger and I went over to him at the double.

The French Army had established a headquarters at Bayeux. I was to go with Philippe on a mission of liaison.

Philippe sat with the French driver of the jeep and I perched in the rear. He explained to me that Bayeux was famous for the tapestries depicting the adventures of William the Conqueror on his invasion of England in 1066.

I gave Philippe a jag from a Scottish thistle.

"Bloody good thing William didn't come up to Scotland. We would have sorted him out."

"Scotland." This from the driver. He shuddered. "The mountains and the rain, *non, non, non, mon Dieu,* for William and me Hastings, Eastbourne, London, *mais oui!*"

Before I could tell him he was a "comic", the driver stabbed the accelerator and the roar of the engine barely covered Philippe's laughter, while we sped over pot-holes, a white cloud of dust rising. I felt the hot wind and sun burn my face like a sirocco.

We made good time. Bayeux was not far away, but far enough from German artillery. We could walk about in relative peace. Two girls in uniform stopped to speak to Philippe. They were young, very attractive and I was glad I had brushed my teeth. I started my big victory leer but it froze half-way of its target. Each of the girls had a coloured ribbon sewn over the left breast pocket of their jackets, the Croix de Guerre. Who was liberating this country? Me or them?

After we had left them I strode beside Philippe, grabbed his arm and yelped, "Hey! What about these two?"

The girls had come from Paris to the coast in an attempt to escape to Britain. The opportunity came. They stole a rowing-boat and pushed out into the sea in darkness. When dawn broke, they had succeeded in rowing a few miles from the French coast. Then all hell broke loose.

The day was 6 June. The guns of the Allied fleet opened up in a tumultuous roar of thunder and blinding lightning flashes as guns blazed a sky trail. Small craft were bobbing on course for the beaches. The girls were in the thick of the Normandy invasion.

In the L.C.A.s approaching, tough, cynical, laconic, poker-faced, crap-playing Americans sat crowded, rhythmically chewing, teeth lacerating gum—the Yanks were coming.

Up front, the coxswain blinked, steadied the helm and his voice, then reported coolly, calmly and crisply, "Gee, Lootenant! Goils!"

As if commanded by a United States Marines' master sergeant, thirty sets of Yankee teeth clamped down hard, ejecting saliva, gum cementing every jaw. Thirty pairs of eyes took on a speculative, interested expression. Thirty heads bobbed up over the gunwales. A hushed chorus, "Goils!"

The two girls had been picked up and brought ashore, landing in foaming surf, through the hail of bullets and the splatter of explosions.

The French two-and-a-half ringer shook hands, offered us a wash and gave us towels. We had lunch and did what we had to do. The French army was re-organizing at speed and would soon be in the field as a force to be reckoned with.

Philippe asked if I had any objection to returning to Hauger by a different route. He wanted to visit an old friend, Madame Fremont, at the Ferme Lasson near Caen.

We left the French driver in Bayeux. Philippe took the wheel and I sat up front shielded by the windscreen. He parked the jeep at the farm entrance and walked forward with his customary sailor's gait although he was on dry land and it was not heaving, to be greeted and worshipped like a pop star. I waited diffidently, in the wings, off stage.

The old lady was obviously Madame Fremont. She was thin, wore a black dress and her grey hair was brushed back and gathered in a bun. She was pulling at Philippe's arm, waggling a finger under his nose and scolding him. She pointed to me and Philippe beckoned me to the group around him.

"She is very angry with me and says I am very bad to leave my friend forgotten and not introduced. She apologizes for the bad manners to you, the honoured guest."

My hand was clasped. There was no need for her to speak. The warm dry pressure of her fingers and the message in her eyes made me welcome to France and to her house.

We gathered in the dining-room, a large airy space, with some heavy old pieces of furniture. There were two tables, one set for the adults, the smaller one, at the bay window, for the children.

Eventually we were seated—Madame, two other younger women, the schoolmaster, the priest, Philippe and myself and a very serious young man of 16 years. Seven children of varying ages laughed and chuckled by the bay window. One, a child of about 12 years, was permitted to sit with the adults. She had learned to speak a little English at school. She was seated beside me. Our conversation was to be serious, but resulted in shoulder-shaking giggles.

A meal of soup, veal and vegetables, followed by fresh fruit and Camembert cheese, with rich red wine flowing in and out of tall glasses, made a banquet.

The serious youth took charge at the head of the table. Every now and then the old lady spoke sharply to Philippe and he turned to me.

"She is worried that you do not have enough to eat."

I patted my tummy and raised my glass to her. She looked happy.

The youth had disappeared only to return reverently holding a bottle in both hands, the way I would caress a bottle of Glenfiddich, Old Bowmore, or Highland Park. The treasure trove was not an old mind-soothing Scots Malt. It was Calvados. Pale golden liquid was poured into tiny liqueur glasses and Philippe stood up to give a toast.

"Who will be a true Norman?"

All tossed the yellow spirit down their throats. I did the same. It was a powerful sensation. There was a sudden shock of fiery fluid burning its way deep into the system to reach my feet and twitch my toes, then surging up and scorching my belly, a furnace of flames reaching my face from a witch's cauldron, creating a hot sun.

I sat down gasping, fighting for breath and croaking hoarsely. If I lived, I would sign the pledge, never again to be a true Norman, to take it easy on the Calvados and stick to Bonnie Scotland and Glenfiddich.

On the way back I asked Philippe, "That young fellow acted like the master in the house. Where is Monsieur Fremont?"

Philippe took his time as he drove and thought.

Monsieur Fremont was one of a French group who helped Allied airmen to escape. He gave sanctuary to pilots who were shot down. He had been caught and the penalty was death. When the firing-squad came, the German officer in command was unhappy. He was a soldier, his war was not aimed at old men, women or children. But for him, orders were orders and must be carried out.

He offered to blindfold Monsieur Fremont but the old Frenchman refused. The German asked him to face the wall, but the old man waved him away scornfully. The German pleaded and entreated but the answer was the same, "*Non!* I am not afraid to die."

The firing-squad lined up, their Mauser rifles aimed to kill, fingers curled round triggers, eyes squinting along V-sights and foresights. Before the volley rang out spitting death, Monsieur Fremont raised his right hand and pointed upwards to heaven. In a clear, calm voice, he spoke distinctly, "*Vive la France.*"

# 10

# Orphan Recruits

At the beginning of July, the commando moved to Breville. We were still in the front-line defensive position which was not the sort of role we had been trained for. We had expected to be withdrawn to take up our task of special operations but so far it had not been found possible to relieve us.

The change from Hauger to Breville brought a sharp attack from the Germans with mortar and small-arms fire. Rifleman Keeley, lying beside the R.S.M., Bill Morris, and myself, was shot. The regimental sergeant-major, tough and gruff, forgot to bawl and shout. Whilst I held Keeley, the R.S.M. got busy with a field-dressing.

Keeley's blue eyes quizzed me.

"Bad is it, sir?"

"Not bad, Keeley. It has gone through the fleshy part of the shoulder. I think it went straight through."

"Blighty is it?" he grinned.

" 'fraid so, Keeley."

"That's alright then. Bow Bells it is for me. I'll go home and see me Mum."

The small village of Breville had some houses still intact. I shrugged off the gremlins. Slit trenches were being dug. Headquarters, Signals and F Troop, occupied the village.

When settled I called for Jock and together we went off to see the two most forward troops. Webby, Gordon Webb, was pleased to see me. His troop had an uncomfortable position, well forward and almost cut off by the terrain of close hedgerows and copses. I was beginning to realize the importance of visiting forward troops even if it was only to tell them that headquarters were still operating in the field and that we had not pushed off to Paris for the weekend.

Patey, Gordon's runner, was brewing up. He was a dark-haired burly character, the Jeeves of B Troop. Sergeant-Major Chattaway completed the group round the tiny fire. Chattaway was a slim, tough, cool customer with experience. He had fought in the Spanish Civil War. He was a "joker", too.

At Troon in Ayrshire, he had attended a Troop Sergeant-

Majors' Conference chaired by the R.S.M., Bill Morris. During the conference, he had played inconsequently with a Mills grenade. As he fiddled about with it, the others had eyed it nervously, but no one had liked to object or show concern.

Suddenly, the grenade slipped from his hands and rolled along the floor. The pin fell out and the lever sprang off to jangle against the table. It started to smoke. With a five-second fuse in an enclosed space, there are few seconds to let live or let die. Some made it over the table, some to the door and some to the window. All except Chattaway—he was rocking with mirth. He had doctored an unfilled training grenade. There was no explosion because he had removed the detonator and left only the fuse to smoke.

The fire Patey was tending did not smoke. Flames curled round the metal pan and the water bubbled. We had a madhatters' tea party. Now was the moment to press on.

Jock and I were only 100 yards away when we heard a whistling whine. The explosion followed so quickly we had no time to duck. Gordon, Patey and Chattaway were picking themselves up from the ground where they had been thrown as if by an unseen hand. The shells had landed immediately behind them. The red-hot metal had been pressurized forward, but the blast had back-fired on the group. They were dusting themselves down and Patey was trying to salvage what was left of the tea. He was muttering unintelligible curses. McCall was sympathetic. It had happened to him and he did not like anyone to spill his "char". That was an unforgivable crime.

Peter King and C Troop were even further forward, in a small copse, as a standing patrol. They were isolated and with hedges and thickets all around, there was little chance to sleep or to relax, constantly straining eyes and ears in the tenseness of complete concentration.

Peter King was now a captain, promoted in the field for his courage and leadership at Hauger, when the troop leader, David Style, had been wounded. I promised him that I would visit C Troop frequently. The troop's position was not to be envied and I would have to try to arrange that they were relieved within a reasonable time.

"Meantime," I asked, "is there anything I can get for you to help make life more bearable?"

"We could do with some books to read."

"O.K. What kind of books would you like?"

He thought for a moment, "Anything really—detective stories—something thrilling."

Good God! Twenty men, stuck out here, the last outpost, suffering shelling, mortaring, dive-bombing and German patrols—and they wanted to read something exciting, like sudden death! Jock and I tottered off.

N.C.O.s of D Troop awaited me at Breville. Tomorrow, they explained, would be Lieutenant John Hunter-Gray's twenty-first birthday. How could they help him to celebrate the event? Headquarters staff vacated a room and biscuits, wine, cigarettes and matches were conjured up out of space. Arrangements were made to relieve members of D Troop, ten at a time.

Hunter-Gray was summoned to headquarters. He arrived in a sweat, unsure whether he was to be caned or promoted. The Colonel wished him a "Happy Birthday" and ushered him into the surprise reception. Perhaps it was not the best time and place to celebrate a twenty-first birthday, but it was one he would remember, if he was capable of remembering anything.

That was my office gone for the day. I might as well go out and visit the crazy gang at F Troop. They had taken two new members on strength. Jock and I would go and look them over.

Troop Sergeant-Major Taffy Edwards had a pugilistic face on top of a burly broad-shouldered figure. He was standing as near to attention as he could, since he had, under each arm, a tortoise-shell-coloured kitten. They had been found, like orphans, alone in the billet, and had been adopted by the troop. They were ready for inspection.

"Private 'Dee Day' and private 'Dee Plus One', sir."

The kittens had also secret code-names, Dawson and Menday, after the colonel and second-in-command. When Len Coulson, Big Mac, and Taffy Edwards felt disgruntled, they worked off their displeasure on "Dawson" and "Menday", marching them in and out, yelping, "Stand at attention when I am speaking to you."

"Dee Day" was particularly bright with a high I.Q. He had been promoted to lance-corporal, acting unpaid. Unfortunately, he had misbehaved and had been reduced to the ranks.

"Caught 'im in the act, sir," Taffy Edwards rapped out, "Put 'im on a B252, conduct contrary to good order and military discipline—pee-ing in the troop leader's green beret."

Len Coulson and Big Mac were looking grimly serious. It was, of course, a serious offence. "Can't have that sort of thing going on," added the sergeant-major. "Before we know where we are, the whole troop will be pee-ing in Cap'n Coulson's green beret."

It was an exit line.

The weather continued to hold good. What it was good for, I wasn't too sure. I reported to the Colonel, and, at that moment, it happened.

A flurry of explosions shook the building, the earth quaked, dust, plaster and masonry drifted about the room. We waited, eyeing each other, expecting the next shock wave. The door burst open. Ken Kennett, the signals corporal, shouldered through. He gasped, "The signals billet has been hit badly." As he turned to go, we were on his heels, the colonel, the R.S.M. and myself.

Most of the house occupied by the Signals Section had been demolished, the roof and walls caving in with the blast. Many hands were already pulling away rubble and frenziedly seeking their pals, dead or wounded.

In a room adjacent, the doctor and orderlies were attending to one of the seriously wounded. The man was laid out on his back on a rough table. A metal clip on one side of his face held the flesh together. He was in a bad way and had been given a shot of morphine.

I recognized him. His name was O'Donnell and was from my home town of Paisley. He was trying to speak. I lit a cigarette and held it so that he could draw on it. His eyes signalled "Thanks," I bent closer to hear him.

"Sir, please make sure I get back to the boys—No. 4 Commando."

I nodded, and he looked content. Robert caught and held my stare. Neither of us could trust ourselves to speak so we busied ourselves with physical action. This chap had a chance. It was all a question of speed back to the regimental aid post, and godspeed to Britain.

Somehow I understood his desire to return. If he wanted to live, love, laugh and die, then this was the place and these were the men that covered all the actions.

Each area raises new problems for operations, whether attacking or defensive. At Breville, while H.Q. and F Troop occupied the village, the other troops were strung out forming a semicircular perimeter facing the Germans like a family of hedgehogs, needle-sharp, not easy to handle when disturbed.

The village was at the edge of a slope which ran down to the plains before Caen. It stood at the very end of high ground dominating all the roads and the valley below. On the other side, thick, wooded, close country stretched away towards the River Dives. We were again in the sort of country we had learned to mistrust, friendly orchards with forbidden apples.

Daylight patrolling was cut to a minimum and, instead, pairs of snipers were used. Their endurance was taxed to the utmost limit. A few against many, succeeding in commando tactics, denying the use of ground to the Germans, annoying and disturbing them.

There were casualties in the sniper ranks. Snipers are highly trained specialists. There is more to it than simply giving a man a rifle with a telescopic sight attached and, anyway, there was a shortage of telescopic sights. A few selected men were sent out with experienced dedicated snipers. Who better to train a sniper, than a sniper?

The Germans observed. And when they did, they dropped a mortar "stonk", a hot curry of blasting explosive in a Krupps wrapping. That stuff spread a blood red stain.

By the middle of August the enemy in the wood opposite began to pull out. It seemed that we could be on the move again soon. A message was received that the unit had to supply a guard for Montgomery's headquarters. A detachment was sent from No. 4 under Len Coulson, together with one from No. 6 Commando.

This guard duty for Monty's headquarters was held to be an honour. It was not the usual ceremonial guard and they were emphatically warned of their responsibilities. They were told that Monty's H.Q. had already been attacked by small groups of Germans who had been cut off by the advancing column and were still capable of operating as raiding parties.

Len and his party went straight into slit trenches on guard duty. They were accustomed to challenging once, then firing if no satisfactory reply was given. So aggressive were they in this business, that various members of staff at Monty's H.Q. were almost scared to go afoot at night without first hailing the nearest sentry to tell him of their intention.

Monty could rest assured that if German troops made a desperate attempt on his life, they would first have to eliminate hard-eyed, icy-cold commando soldiers.

As fair exchange, the General showed his confidence in his guard. He intrigued and pleased them by his trust. They were intelligent and they were entitled to know what was going on in this great big war. Monty made sure that they did. Each day, a high-ranking staff officer showed the guard Monty's war map, explained what was happening, and what he, the General, intended to do about it.

Our own leaders had always recognized that to get a job well done, it was necessary to tell the troops, in detail, all the information. That way they could dish up their own devil's brew. Monty, by showing the common soldier touch, won their hearts. For them, as it was for him, it was "nae bother at aw' ".

Back at Breville, the remainder of No. 4 Commando had not long to wait. The Allied front, so long static, was about to burst into action. The main thrust was to be delivered by armoured and motorized columns in a superb sweep to the Rhine. Falaise would become the burial ground of an entire German army. The irrepressible "Blood and guts" Patton would lead American armour in a phenomenal dash across France, culminating in an historic message to "Ike", General Eisenhower, as Patton stood by the Rhine.

On the morning of 18 August, Monty was ready to move. The 21st Army Group was about to be unleashed. We would again lead No. 1 Special Service Brigade, to break out and race for the high ground at the Dives, a commanding position from which the German gunners had a grandstand view. Brigadier Mills-Roberts had issued his orders. His plan was different. He was good at cutting red tape, now he gave us white tape. The attack was mounted at night. The commando spearhead was to be thrown forward laying a white cable which the whole brigade would follow.

Dawn broke, and we were well on our way, helped by a creeping barrage of death conjured up by the Royal Artillery. German tanks and S.P. vehicles lay burning and smoking, hot metal incinerators from which there had been no escape. Grey uniformed bodies of infantrymen, charred and unrecognizable humans, lay in curious poses of death. Fallen trees, stripped of branches and bark, and scorched hedgerows completed the scene.

Mills-Roberts was pleased with the white tape idea. He would do the same thing again. Later, the brigade was to infiltrate the enemy lines at night with an unusual result.

At first light, brigade headquarters found that they were about to shave, wash and eat breakfast with the Germans. In the lower echelon we had chuckled over the lurid account.

We had all recognized that to be on the staff at brigade, one had to be a gentleman, crisp, polite and intelligent. They gave the impression of the good life of bath, shave, haircut and manicure. We had known better than to accept their cover. This batch we had at brigade were a lot of nice, charming bloody-minded bastards, who would cut a throat with an apologetic smile.

Now, confronted with the Germans, someone made his cocktail party remark, "My dear! Who are these awful people?"

With the Brigadier bellowing and brandishing his shillelagh, his staff forgot their languid poise and bayoneted, knifed and throttled every German in sight. An epic in hand-to-hand combat.

Tony Lewis, who had taken over No. 6 Commando when Derek Mills-Roberts had been made brigadier, had similar ideas. His R.T. set had crackled as the Brigadier spat his order "Tony—take the bridge."

No. 6 Commando had crawled into a position at the edge of a wood to face the foe. Bren-guns placed at a flank, started to chatter. Ryan Price, the adjutant, stood up and blew "tally-ho" on a hunting horn. No. 6 Commando had dashed forward, to stamp out all resistance in a wave of steel.

No. 1 S.S. Brigade was on it way towards its goal. The brigade would return to Britain on 6 September 1944. Some operational changes would be made.

Captain John Thompson would go back to hospital. He would have a tale to tell. He was fair, not bad-looking if you disregarded his nose which was squashed as flat as a proboscis ironed out by a steam-roller.

John had come down from Peterhouse, Cambridge, where he was an open scholar taking science in 1939. He had been awarded a Ministry of Agriculture scholarship to the Royal Dick Veterinary College in Edinburgh, where he was to work on certain diseases of sheep.

In October 1939, he joined the Scots Guards as a Guardsman. Eventually, he was sent to Sandhurst and commissioned in his father's old regiment, the South Wales Borderers. He volunteered for special service and was posted to No. 4 Commando, transferring to No. 6 Commando in 1943 at Brighton.

On D-Day plus 5, he was given the task of leading a large fighting patrol of the 12th (Yorkshire) Battalion Parachute Regiment into Breville Wood. On reaching the starting line all hell erupted. John and the leading troops were suddenly lambasted by artillery, not only from the Germans but also from their own gunners firing short. The whine, noise and crump of high explosives was deafening. John took cover beside a small group of paratroopers.

At this moment all his training came to the fore. He remembered a Sandhurst lecture on "officer-like qualities" and similar topics. Here was his opportunity. He addressed himself to his neighbours. At that moment, they were curled up in an attempt to reduce their size to tiny insignificant targets. They raised themselves slightly at the crisp words of an officer trying out the qualities.

"Don't worry chaps! Everything will be alright!"

A tremendous flurry of explosions followed causing a hail of burnt jagged metal. All the group were severely hit, including John Thompson. They were evacuated to a hospital near Arromanches. It was in darkness and the place was being mortared. They were packed together like sardines. Still, it was worth giving Sandhurst, the training and the lectures another try so John turned to his neighbour, who was but a dark shadowy form and started to speak.

"Things might be worse, y'know."

The bulky figure moved, turning so that John could see the whites of two eyes and the gleam of teeth signalling a reply.

"Excuse me, sir, I can recognize your voice. Aren't you the officer who told us that everything was going to be alright?"

Gordon Webb would be promoted to Major and posted with others to the Holding Operational Commando at Wrexham. I would go to the Commando Basic Training Centre—the commandant, Charles Vaughan, had asked for me. Jock McCall would go also.

These changes meant that battle experience recently gained could be passed on, releasing others at the H.O.C. and the C.B.T.C. for operations. More and more campaign ribbons would be seen by recruits who eyed these with respect.

There was another significant change. Commandos were originally recruited from army volunteers, but now Royal Marine

Commando Units were increasing in number. They were a regular force and would eventually take over the role of commandos, since the administration of men from numerous different regiments created problems. No. 4 Commando would join with Nos 41, 47 and 48 Royal Marine Commandos in No. 4 S.S. Brigade for their sledge-hammer assault on Walcheren and Flushing in Holland.

Few commandos, if any, were in every action. Numbers were restricted by the type of operation and craft used. A green beret was like an international team blazer. The wearer was in the squad or club, picked to play when he was needed.

I now knew what was in store for Jock and me; I began retracing in my mind the fate-ordained steps that had brought me to this stage in my life.

A link . . . a chain of events
. . . one "damp" thing after another

# 11

# Achnacarry

It had taken me four and a half years and special training to get on board an invasion ship. This is how it happened.

My pals were all in the armed services. The girls had gone into uniform. Those who had stepped out of it were strictly married.

Was I really a quiet, peaceable penpusher or was I a swashbuckling hell-raiser? Could it be that I now had the image of these other commandos—tough, saturated in experience, from whom husbands hid their wives, while mothers wept over their daughters?

If I had gone through a transformation, it had not happened overnight.

On 3 September 1939, war was declared. I dropped my banker's pen and took up a sword.

A year earlier with a close friend, Arnott Cochran, who had a draper's business in Paisley, I had joined the Territorial Army, commissioned into the 9th Battalion, The Cameronians (Scottish Rifles). We had the faint hope that a show of determination to fight might dissuade Hitler from his purpose. But ranting, raving and shaking his fist, like the lunatic he was, Hitler was not deterred.

As I left the tiny branch of the bank at the corner of Canal Street, Renfrew, I took a long lingering look. Bold lettering proclaimed proudly "Royal Bank of Scotland". Below, on an oblong piece of cardboard, hooked by string to a drawing-pin stuck in the woodwork, was a notice. Printed as bravely as a *Scottish Daily Express* front-page headline, it stated, "Foreign Business Transacted Here".

Little did I know the sort of foreign business I was about to transact. First came the training, route-marching, map-reading and a variety of courses for junior commanders in the British

Army. Suddenly, we were not toy soldiers any more. German Panzers, armoured tank divisions, had swept through the Low Countries to penetrate the defences of the British Expeditionary Force and Allies on the Continent.

Between 27 May and 4 June 1940, 338,266 British and 26,175 French troops succeeded in escaping German pincers and landed in England. This had involved every conceivable size and shape of ship in a desperate rescue bid.

With my unit, in 45 Brigade, 15th Scottish Division, I found myself commanding A Company of 120 men, with the task of guarding the shore at Thorpeness, on the Naze, in Essex.

From the sun's rays or misty cloud, R.A.F. hawks released from airfield wrists swooped to kill. Winged men spun, spiralled and plummeted. The sky was alive, glinting silver and blue, while we watched death come to R.A.F. "angels" in a light-shattering burst of stardom in the Battle of Britain.

Standing to, in the gun-pits, there was a sense of frustration. The fight of the "Few" against the many, only broken from us by a hysterical outburst of machine-gun fire aimed at low-flying Germans, strafing the beach.

My secondment was a War Office posting to help start off the new Royal Air Force Regiment. Army officers took over responsibility for training at Filey, Yorkshire, in Billy Butlin's camp. Instead of Billy's redcoats, army sergeants bawled, "Wakey! Wakey! Rise and shine", and swore great oaths at "erks" who failed to stick a bayonet through the dummy, hanging limply like a hunk of dead meat between narrow gallows.

When trained, the R.A.F. Regiment would guard airfields and release army "bods" more used to fire and movement. A flight consisted of about 200 men and there were two flights in a squadron, commanded by a major. I had a flight.

The major, Smith, was much older, had thin, greying hair and neat moustache. He was impeccably dressed and precise in speech. He had seen service on the North-West Frontier of India. He was proud of his youthful son, a midshipman in the Royal Navy on a battleship. He could not understand why a young fellow like me was not in the thick of the fighting, and said so.

This was all too true. My assault training and unarmed combat account was in the red, with no credits due. Not even a submission from a wrestling "Wren" or a wriggling "Waaf". It was high time I threw my weight around, all ten stones, and became more aggressive.

A sergeant, a Royal Scots Fusilier, a boxing type called Fulton, needed a sparring partner. Rumour had it that he was a champion. He proved it to me.

In a flurry of blows, I saw blood ooze from his mouth. It was not my blood. Then I was floored, peeping out of one eye. My lower lip was swelling into a chipolata sausage with a petulant look. Fulton was kneeling beside me, contrite, apologetic and sympathetic. He knew that tomorrow I was to be best man at the R.A.F. padre's wedding. Raw meat was rationed so he had to use his portion on my eye, and cook and eat the steak afterwards.

Horror showed on the bridesmaid's face. She had never seen a best man like me before and I did not feel up to joking like Tony Galento, not when I had a lip as big and coloured as a fairground balloon. The photographer shuffled me into the guest pack as smoothly as a card-sharp losing an unwanted knave.

Back at Filey, the major confronted me. I groaned and pointed to my wounds. "See, I've been in the wars. I don't think I'll live." He was amused. He would be the death of me, if he did not die laughing first.

"Why don't you apply for the Indian Army?"

He did not mean the "redskins", but those other marvellous warriors, the Bengal Lancers, the Punjabis or the Gurkhas. The latter were very handy with a curved sickle knife called a *kukri*.

While I waited for an answer from the India Office, Smith, like the wall squiggle "Kilroy", was here. Excitedly he stuck a folded newspaper in front of my nose and jabbed a finger at the picture staring me in the eyes. The men wore curious woollen caps. They were dressed in lightweight denim battledress and festooned with weapons. Faces smeared with black, accentuated grinning, ivory-white teeth.

This could not be a black and white minstrel show. The caption spelled "Commandos" which was from a Boer War Afrikaans word, *Kommando*, meaning a swift, lightly-armed cavalry column.

These men, British commandos, had raided the Lofoten Islands off Norway and personified success.

"That's what you should be in."

With the major I could get writer's cramp. I wrote and within a week, I was on my way to an interview at Adamton House, near

Prestwick, in Scotland—only a couple of miles from my home today, forty years later.

The guard was big, broad and burly, an unsmiling bruiser with cold blue eyes. His feet were cemented to the terrazzo as firmly as Atlas on his pedestal. Arms were clamped to his sides, exactly in line with the seams of his crease-stiff battle dress. The palm of his right hand hovered over the butt of a low-slung Colt automatic tucked into a holster, buckled to his thigh above the knee.

After going through the security sieve, I was shown into a room two flights upstairs. Four officers lolled languidly in chairs behind a long table. They looked thoroughly bored and uninterested.

I crashed my feet on bare boards. My right hand whistled through the air in salute. Sunlight through the window twinkled on the silver Douglas star on my Glengarry, the silken tails of which flowed behind in battle-honour pride. Rays of light beamed from the black brogues peeping out beneath blue-green and white checked tartan trews. A shining display of Cameronian covenanting might.

The officers were shocked, stunned, suffering agonizing pain. One shaded his eyes with a limp hand, while another, elbows on table, gently pressed at his temples with two fingers of each hand.

Recovery was slow, a tedious business, with questions.

"What sports do you play?"

"Do you drink beer?"

"Can you swim?"

"Do you play a musical instrument?"

"Do you have a sex life?"

"Were you a Boy Scout?"

I answered as truthfully as possible and at last I was dismissed in an atmosphere of mutual relief. I feared the worst.

Much to my surprise, I was accepted. Smith was delighted but I growled with second thoughts. I told him that it was a condition of acceptance that all ranks volunteering for special service had to revert to their war substantive rank. That meant I would no longer be a captain. I would lose a "pip" and become a lieutenant. Even at that, my sacrifice was relatively small. To get into commando service, sergeant-majors voluntarily became privates. Greater love hath no man, a sergeant-major, than that.

Smith produced a map. The instructions were to report to the

Commando Basic Training Centre at Achnacarry, near Spean Bridge, by Fort William, in Lochaber, Inverness-shire.

The search took time, but we found it. Achnacarry was not really near anywhere. There were golden eagles up there. The eagles were lucky, they had eyes to mark the spot.

Achnacarry House is the home of Cameron of Lochiel, the chief of Clan Cameron, and stands beside the River Arkaig which stretches for only a mile or so, connecting Loch Arkaig to Loch Lochy, both fathomless depths. *Aig* is a Norse word meaning bay, hence Mallaig, or Mal-a-Vik, eel bay. Vikings in longships had prowled along these shores.

Lochaber was full of romantic history of the '15 and '45 rebellions, Bonnie Prince Charlie and heroes like Banquo, Donhul Dhu, and Sir Ewen of Lochiel. Sir Ewen in a feat of unarmed combat had bitten through the throat of his opponent, an English officer, and was afterwards heard to say, that it was the best bite he had had in a lifetime. In olden days, wolves had roamed the Lochaber countryside. It seemed a likely place to breed some more.

The short period of leave at home actually palled. I was secretly glad to take the road to the Isles, by Tummel and Loch Rannoch and Lochaber. I would go to Spean Bridge.

As the train clanked to a steam-hissing halt to have a quiet smoke out of the stack, the sound of the bagpipes echoed in the station at the edge of the tiny village. Officers and men of many different regiments filled the platform. In the distance, Ben Nevis, 4,406 feet above sea level, frowned and shed misty tears, not for us, but for the tall thin-faced adjutant of the C.B.T.C. His name was Joy but nobody laughed.

We were herded across the hump-backed railway bridge by instructors who stood out, dressed in camouflaged two shade green jackets. Their equipment was blancoed white with brasses burnished and they were wearing green berets.

Then the shock. No transport.

"Who needs transport?" they asked. "It's only a short walk— seven miles."

It was raining, but we had waterproof gascapes and we had a pied piper—Pipe-Major MacLaughlan. We followed as he started to play and march into the hills and glens. A squelching, water-logged legion of the damned, already lost.

By the time we had reached the gates at the tree-lined avenue to

Achnacarry House, we had absorbed a flood of drizzly rain that made us human sponges. We eyed the mock graves by the gates, the crosses on which bore inscriptions—rank, number and name and "He showed himself on the skyline" or "He failed to take cover on the night assault landing". Had there been space for a communal trench, we would have fallen in and ended the matter there and then.

From where we stood, we could see the concrete which had been poured on parkland to make a "square". Drill sergeants, with pacesticks, were barking, hounding squads of trainee sheep. To one side of the "square" stood Nissen huts, tunnel-shaped huts of corrugated iron with cement floors, named after their inventor.

Nearby, outside the camp, small groups were climbing a steep rock-face, while others were abseiling on a slender strand of rope, floating down as if secured on a bos'n's chair.

Yelps from voices in distress pierced the air and a sergeant remarked, "It's only some stupid man falling off the 'toggle bridge' or the 'Tarzan' course. He has no need to worry, he can go through the course again after he gets back from hospital."

Then, seeing the unspoken question in our eyes, he added, "We've got a hospital at Onich about twenty miles away, at the other side of Fort William. They're good at sticking broken bones together, they are. Get plenty of practice. Send them back quickly, they do. Don't want anyone to miss the fun, they don't."

The sergeant's remarks had barely time to sink in before we were confronted by the commandant, Lieutenant-Colonel Charles Vaughan.

His face was florid but fit looking. His chin was square and his eyes were pale blue. His hair was greying and there was not much of it. With what he had, he had done his best and you would not have called him bald. His voice was throaty, even fatherly. We were not misled. He had been a regimental sergeant-major in the Coldstream Guards, therefore, he would know everything about everything.

Here was the place and moment for rebirth. We would be reborn and baptized with the hellish sounds of bombs, bullets and bawls, screams resounding into the hills, along deep glens, over bracken and heather, above the tumbling rush and roar of torrential rivers.

Anointed into special service by the Grand Lama of these

mountains, we would get wedded to a commando unit. No signet ring would seal the bond, but a green beret would show allegiance. The marriage would be legally binding, all of us being of age, if not of sound mind, joined together, from this day on, forever, for better or worse till death do us part!

## 12

# Gallowglasses—with a Pact

What with the weather up here and the training, death could part us very soon.

Complaining about Vaughan and his instructors and the quantity and rate at which they used live ammunition, a senior staff officer in Whitehall had muttered, "If this goes on much longer, we'll have nothing left for the invasion."

The weather in June 1942 was better. The rain was softer. Earlier, in January and February, the thirty-six-hour scheme had been a hail-storming nightmare. We had suffered snowfalls and finally cold, icy rain.

One day I was officer responsible for climbing instruction, at the cliff face, only a short distance away from the castle. Little shrubs and stunted trees sprouted from clefts in the rock. The top was not very high, eighty feet or so, not as stiff a climb as Kilimanjaro, but still a long way to fall. The sergeant instructor was an expert, his name was Leach. In peacetime, he enjoyed scaling all the heights in the Lake District in the North of England. He was nicknamed "Spider" for obvious reasons, and, for obvious reasons, I let him do the talking and the training.

Vaughan came striding towards us with another officer. I prepared to receive them knowing that I need not call the squad to attention. Nothing, not anything nor anyone, stopped the training at Achnacarry.

The officer with Vaughan was very tall, debonair and handsome. I had seen a newspaper photograph of him. Already a legendary figure, a gallant, distinguished leader of men, who had led his troops in seaborne raids at Lofoten and Boulogne. He was wearing a green beret with the silver badge of the Lovat Scouts.

There was no mistaking the Chief of Clan Fraser, Lord Lovat.

I saluted. He chatted and asked questions. I answered. When he went away I watched his long gait enviously, a Highlander's pace which would take hills, rivers and obstacles in its stride.

A few days later, summoned to appear before the colonel, I checked my turn-out along with my possible misdeeds. He looked sad and he spoke almost apologetically.

"Donald, I am sorry to tell you this, you've been posted to a Commando unit stationed at Troon, No. 4 Commando. Lord Lovat is your new C.O."

Vaughan was doing his best to soften this tragic blow. Trying to keep a note of envy from his voice, he added, "You're on a good thing now, Donald, eh? Civvy billets and easy living."

Endeavouring to hide pleasurable excitement, I escaped to my room to pack. I paused to look out of the window of the castle to see the mist swirl around shadowy figures and to hear the bawls and shouts. An echo from the past.

Long ago, on 31 January 1645, a bloody battle had been fought at Inverlochy, near Fort William, eighteen miles away, when Montrose and his Royalist Highlanders had carried out a commando operation. A flank march in a hyperborean hell of snow and ice, through mountain passes, in darkness, at speed, to gain surprise. At dawn on 2 February, Montrose had fallen on the Campbells, glutted with reiving and burning in Glen Spean and Glen Roy. The piobh mhor had screamed for vengeance.

I felt a shiver of ice trickling down my spine. Vaughan was right. It was, as he said "an 'elluva country!" A country fit to train a superb, super-confident fighting force—commandos! Now I was on my way to join one.

My arrival at Troon in Ayrshire, with a batch of newly fledged commandos, was not greeted with a brass band. No. 4 Commando did not blow trumpets. Their instruments heralded the last day of summer for the Germans, and their icy smiles that winter for the enemy would be cold and harrowing.

On Monday, we were inoculated and vaccinated. On Tuesday, we were swimming for the shore, and our lives, off Arran. The larger type of craft had been used, Landing-Craft Infantry. Every precaution is taken in exercises but the element of risk is always there. Unlike the small assault landing-craft we had used, the bigger vessels had difficulty in getting close inshore and the chances of broaching to were greater. When the ramps went down we dashed off, eager to hit the shallows and race up the beach. As a result, we found ourselves in the sea, out of our depth, holding on to rifles, tommy-guns and bren-guns, and floundering.

Despite efforts to cling to the craft and hook arms and legs around poor swimmers, two men had been drowned. They had clung to one another, unwilling to let the other go under, weapons looped over their heads, hampering movement and weighing them down. Two commando soldiers, pals, taking the rough with the smooth, sticking together to the end. A tragedy, but one which brought us together, evidence of the close companionship of commandos, comrades in arms. A bond had been forged.

The commando was moved south to Weymouth. Training continued. Major Mills-Roberts bawled at us until we got it right—the contours of the ground, timing and speed. Weapons were fired and checked. Demolition charges prepared. Maps, aerial photographs and a sand-table model pored over. Meticulously, we were briefed with our eyes on a German gun-battery. As excitement mounted, sceptical old soldiers warned me, "It probably won't come off. We've been through all this before, training and training for an operation which might be cancelled. We'll believe it when we see it."

Then I saw them. A group of happy, grinning commandos walking in the warm sunshine. They were carrying bundles of bayonets, newly cleaned and sharpened—British steel, Sheffield made, guaranteed to do the job.

The job, the Dieppe raid, was about to be done.

We landed at dawn. As assault craft seared the sandy shallows, the ramps went down. The Germans, rudely wakened, feverishly opened up with mortars and machine-guns but they were too late.

Commandos scattered up the beach. Already bangalore torpedoes had blown gaps in the barbed-wire defences. Others, wearing leather jackets, threw themselves on to the barbed obstacles to make human bridges over which we ran.

Lovat led us jauntily, dressed in corduroy slacks and a grey woollen sweater with 'Lovat' sewn across it. A Winchester sporting rifle was slung over his shoulder.

Going like sprinters for the tape, we hared under the flaming arc of enemy machine-gun bullets. We knew where we were, we knew where we were going. Major Mills-Roberts had not spared us when training nor had he spared himself. This was the "pay-off"—for the Germans!

With Lovat up front, leading us on, encouraging and exhorting, and with the help of the R.A.F. Boston aircraft flying low and strafing the enemy gun-site, B Troop slipped quietly round to the rear. Small groups stalking, hard-eyed, out for the kill.

The assault came. Bayonets, tommy-guns, knives and butts of rifles tore the guts out of the German gun-battery at Varengeville.

Jimmy McKay, the demolition officer, was rubbing his hands and muttering, "Fit like a glove, fit like a glove." He was referring to the specially made-up charges of explosive he had stuck up the breeches of the guns, before touching off the fuse. As if in a trance, he went on talking.

"Scrap—scrap metal—even Krupps won't be able to repair that lot."

How we had got to know the calibre of the guns and the exact size of the breeches was a mystery. I had heard of the Free French Forces of the Interior and their resistance movement. The reports were the stuff that thrillers are made of. But were there people who actually accepted the risks to themselves, their friends and their families? I did not get time to ask or find out.

Lovat was commanding like a Highland chief unleashing his clansmen, "Burn the lot". Then there was burning, reiving and spoiling at the German gun-site at Varengeville. Flames licked at buildings. A black pall of smoke pirouetted. There was the poisonous smell of cordite, death and destruction.

At the guns there had been another brief encounter, a fleeting moment in the midst of battle. In the smoke haze and the wild madness of men in fury, we saw him.

The shot came from the barn and cut our comrade down. A German came out and used his boots on the wounded man. Our weapons came up, but were stayed by the hand of the corporal. Coolly he aimed and squeezed the trigger. We watched stonily as the German screeched and clawed at his guts.

Then we were there. For the beast, a bayonet, and the group, Marshall, Keeley and Hurd, knelt beside me. I got out the syringe, checked the dose and cleaned the flesh which Keeley had bared in readiness. The needle went in and the morphine too.

Medical orderlies could not be expected to be everywhere. They accepted the same risks as all of us. To help out some of us were trained, and I had experience. My mother had suffered from diabetes. She had been able, for a time, to do her own injections. Then she had asked me. I was young, so I had to swallow a lump in my throat and nod, "Yes I'll do it." She had trained me to some purpose.

In the commando, we had made a pact among ourselves never to leave our wounded in the field alone, and to do our best always to take them back with us from raids. Hitler had issued an order that all commandos were to be destroyed, whether with weapons or without, or even if "these creatures" showed readiness to surrender, they were to be shown no mercy.

Not that we had ever asked for mercy or expected any. Commandos were tough, as tough as the ancient Scottish mercenary soldiers, "Gallowglasses" who took their name from the huge axes they wielded in battle. They were the most renowned force of their time and sought by every commander waging war on the Continent. They had made a pact among themselves never to leave a battlefield defeated.

We had promised. We had to take this man back with us.

Major Mills-Roberts barked at me, "Lead the way back to the beach." I took my life in my hands and summoned up nervous strength. He was not only a major, but an officer of the Guards, the Irish Guards. So I hesitated. "My section sergeant, Watkins, and this man are wounded. I . . ."

My voice was drowned as he blasted me with his roar, "Get going" and as I turned he added, "they'll be looked after." Mills-Roberts had promised. With Marshall, Keeley and Hurd still with me, I started for the beach, leaving behind a funeral pyre.

Sergeant Watkins got back to Britain and recovered. The wounded man I had attended to was taken aboard an L.C.A. and transferred out at sea to a destroyer, for immediate attention in the sick bay. The destroyer was dive-bombed and among those killed was our wounded companion.

He did not die in vain. He had trained, lived, fought like a soldier, a commando soldier in special service. Perhaps he did not know, before he died, that we had tried to get him back to England, that we had kept our promise.

But I knew. Marshall, Keeley and Hurd knew. Mills-Roberts and others knew. It was understood, We, all of us, No. 4 Commando, would never leave a field defeated—we would keep our pact!

# 13

## "On Commando"

From Troon, the unit moved to Winchester, an old cathedral town, famous for its public school, and the home of the Rifle Brigade. Sunlight after rain glinted and sparkled on walls made of flint. While we bathed in the sunshine of our action in the Dieppe raid, high up, the operation itself was labelled a disaster for the Canadians had suffered dreadful losses.

The other commando in the raid, whose task was similar to our own, but north of Dieppe, had suffered too. Their small craft had been dispersed by enemy action at sea. But a handful under Lieutenant-Colonel Peter Young and Lieutenant Ruxton had managed to swim ashore. They sniped at the German gun-battery to such effect that the Germans lowered the sights of their huge guns to "snipe" back. This peculiar battle went on all day and prevented the German guns from firing on the main landing at Dieppe.

We were sorry for the Canadians. They had made a direct frontal assault from the sea on a heavily defended town. They had taken a mauling, but they must have done a bit of mauling themselves. No one could tell us otherwise. Canadians were tough and wanted to be "in it". War-wolves from the Rockies could not be caged in Britain. Somehow, sometime, they had to break out. They broke out and broke in, at Dieppe.

Headlines howled in a Calgary newspaper, "Where is the shame and where is the glory?" which are a couple of things a soldier gets no time to think about. Given time, he has other thoughts.

The operation proved that a large-scale landing was not impossible. If Canadian effort and sacrifice were not to be in vain, we had to learn the lessons, train harder, become dedicated, for the day that must surely come—invasion. Canadians had opened the door to let us see what lay beyond. We could do them the honour, accept the invitation and go through. I hoped I might go. And if I did, I would not forget to salute!

Meanwhile, as contenders for a European title, we started training, to stay in the peak of condition and keep in the eyes of war promoters. Would-be champions needed sparring partners. We had each other.

In the absence of Pat Porteous, V.C., who was recuperating from a wound received on the Dieppe raid, I took over temporary command of D Troop. It was the season for "on commando". Each troop leader was allowed to take his men to a town or place of his choosing for two weeks, and to carry out his own brand of training, without any interference from commando headquarters. The troop chose Buxton for a week and Scarborough for a week. The move from one town to another could be engineered into an initiative test.

We gave a field-firing demonstration to the Home Guard. To make it realistic, I arranged for Sergeant Portman to make a demolition, a big bang. He blew a hole the size of a bomb crater.

There were a general and brigadier present, watching. By the look on their faces, I could be locked up by one and congratulated by the other.

The Home Guard at Buxton were well organized. They had a motorized column and a troop of cavalry. Commandos never underestimated these cunning old soldiers who popped up from odd places armed with paper bags filled with plaster or horse manure. Buxton Home Guard had enjoyed our field-firing demonstration. Now they wanted to take on D Troop, in an exercise.

The troop was in position at high speed, acting as enemy paratroopers with their objective an electricity sub-station at a crossroads. Harried right and left by Home Guard cavalry, and with roads denied to us by their motorized column, we were sweating when we prepared our token demolition.

At that moment, the brigadier, acting as umpire, arrived on a high-stepping horse. I turned to stop the man about to throw a bakelite grenade to simulate the big bang. Too late. There was a loud explosion. The brigadier's horse reared, whinnying in fear. The rider fought to control the bucking back and lashing feet. Then it was off, bolting, with the brigadier low over the saddle and hanging on like grim death. There was a pregnant silence. Already I was coining phrases for the letter of apology I would have to write.

Later the brigadier told us that the horse had not stopped until safely back in the stable. He had almost had his head knocked off as the horse galloped in under the lintel foaming at the mouth.

The brigadier had enjoyed the experience, but was doubtful if he would enjoy it again.

I kept the orders short.

"You have forty-eight hours to get to Scarborough. Dress F.S.M.O.—rifles—report at Scarborough station with the address of your billet—you will be clean, smart, and there will be a rifle inspection—The police and Home Guard have been warned to stop you *en route* and if caught you will be held for two hours—pocket money is limited to ten shillings."

Sergeant-Major Carl Carlisle, I and two others had to move the baggage—sixty kit-bags, bren-guns, anti-tank rifle, mortar bombs and ammunition.

Every man reported on time. Some had been chased by police and Home Guard in and out of Marks & Spencers stores, public lavatories and other strange places. One or two had received help from motorists and truck drivers, while a few had slipped through the defences of the railway system. One man arrived at the outskirts of Scarborough on the same day as he had left Buxton. A farmer and his wife gave him food and a bed. They gave him a job and paid him for doing it.

Scarborough Castle seemed impregnable, standing on a grassy rock pinnacle, with high thick walls towering upwards to ancient battlements. This was our target for tonight. The yeomen of the Home Guard of Scarborough would defend it.

Knyvet Carr had entered into the initiative test with enthusiasm. He was obviously the chap to make a feint attack on the main gates and portcullis of the castle, while, with the other section I would attempt to scale the walls and assault the battlements.

As darkness fell, we waited, silent, faces blackened and ready to steal up the rocky, scrubby bank.

Explosions erupted. Knyvet and his merry men were throwing bakelite grenades and letting off thunderflashes. They were creating such a racket, that it was later reported the good people of Scarborough thought an air-raid was in progress.

It was now our turn to go. I stared upwards and wondered if this was the way it happened to Ivanhoe. To the seaward, dannert wire sealed off a minefield. We went as close as we dared. By the time I had scrambled up the slippery slope, Tudor was already perched high on the masonry.

Several toggle ropes were being threaded, the wooden peg at

one end going through the eyehole of another, to make one long line. Moments later we were over, hidden in the shadows and moving catlike towards our objective.

There were no Home Guard look-outs. Why should there be? The great bastion of Scarborough Castle was impregnable and the walls impossible to scale. Except to men like Tudor, Maybury and Meek. Impossible was a word they did not understand.

Unseen and unheard, we mingled with the Home Guard, tapped their shoulders and whispered, "Let's go home now, we're thirsty."

The Home Guard insisted that the commandos were transported to the Drill Hall in their coal lorries, bakers' vans and milk floats, while they themselves marched. A feast of tea, beer and hot pies had been set out. Old soldiers and young commandos were as one, telling tales, bridging the generation gap.

Since I had been at one time seconded to the R.A.F. Regiment at Butlin's Camp in Filey, near Scarborough, it was easy to fix up a field-firing practice in exchange for giving a demonstration.

The troop would attack a pillbox at the edge of the cliff. Our live rounds would arc towards the sea. Gunner Mills and his small group would fire the 2-inch mortars, mixing explosive with smoke charges.

Fire and movement brought us to the final assault. Sergeant Portman and two others were ready to go in under cover of the smoke screen to lay a pole-charge, an explosive device shaped like a carpet sweeper, up against the concrete face of the pillbox.

A message was handed to me. Gunner Mills had been wounded. I raced back. The field-dressing had been applied. Mills was apologetic.

"Sorry sir, I reckon I'm the best in No. 4 Commando with a 2-inch mortar, but I went too far under this tree to get cover to hide the position. I misjudged it and hit a branch of the overhanging foliage, I've got a piece of metal in my back."

With live ammunition the risk of injury was always present. A tiny human error could have a damaging result. Luckily Mills was not too badly wounded but was sent off to hospital.

I sprinted to be on time to see Portman and his group make their token demolition. They flitted out of the blue-grey smoke haze shrouding the pillbox and signalled "Get down".

A loud bang echoed and re-echoed in my eardrums. Black dust spiralled. The explosion sounded bigger than a token charge. I checked. I was still in one piece, others were rising from the ground. On my feet, I joined an army colonel and several R.A.F. officers. Dismay and horror was written all over their faces. I saw what they saw.

A huge, deep, jagged crack zigzagged down the thick concrete. The pillbox sagged to one side in an Admiral Beatty tilt, and the black-browed colonel was muttering, "They've done more damage here in two seconds than the Germans have done in the whole war."

Portman was enthusiastically showing the troop his craftsman's handiwork. Flabbergasted, I squinted, looking for an escape route. The sergeant barked, "Concrete pillboxes breed concrete minds. None shall escape me."

D Troop retired in good order.

---

## 14

## "Brandyballs"

When Pat Porteous, V.C. came back, I was made a captain and given command of E Troop. Almost at once I was allowed to take them "on commando", to Minehead in Somerset. This would help us to get to know each other, and there was a tank regiment in that town.

The squadron commander agreed. His tank crews would fire live shells over the heads of E Troop and give us battle experience. We would be able to crawl about towards a target. If anyone got his head knocked off by an armour-piercing shell he could be told later that he was stupid to stand up when a tank regiment was throwing its confetti.

Afterwards E Troop would be allowed to fire live "303" at the tanks. Armour-piercing shells from the anti-tank rifle would not be permitted. The squadron commander explained apologetically, "Those things make holes and cause a nasty draught."

Our turn came. As the tanks roared past, bren-guns and rifles spewed their sickness as live bullets sped to hit the targets. Never had there been such fun, blasting off at real, live, moving objects.

The squadron commander was gloomy and crestfallen. Testily,

I wondered, what had happened now? I asked him, "What's the matter?"

"Oh! I forgot to take my clothes out of the bin."

"Bin? What bin?"

"The bin at the rear of my tank. It's very light metal y'know. All my kit was in it. Your chaps hit it with everything and the bullets went right through. My gear looks as if it has been attacked by woodworm or a lot of lustful locusts."

Lieutenant Hutch Burt was a red-haired, red-faced Scot. A red handle-bar moustache added to the fierce glare of frosty blue eyes. Hutch had been a drill sergeant in Lord Lovat's company in the Scots Guards. With his help, experience and antics, the troop would be drilled to perfection. They loved it. Hutch was a character.

For the two weeks at Minehead, Hutch asked me not to inspect the troop nor to take notice of anything that seemed unusual. He and the troop had surprises in store for me.

They were lined up, ready for inspection. With Hutch Burt and Sergeant-Major Heaynes in attendance, I walked through the ranks. Every man had grown a moustache varying in shape, size and colour. There were large bushy moustaches, sexy ones, droopy ones, some Mexican bandit moustaches, curly, walrus, crooked, some pencil thin and others of a fuzzy nature. I admired each one. They were finding it difficult. Lips were twitching, holding back broad, beaming grins.

Symes had a thin black pencil line of hair on his upper lip. I passed on, stopped and went back. There was something different about Symes. I was conscious that the whole troop was agog. What was it, I wondered?

He was not the usual specimen conjured up, of a rough, tough diamond of a commando soldier. On the contrary, he was pale, thin, weedy, had sunken cheeks sad eyes and was deformed. One shoulder was much lower than the other.

Yet it was he who insisted on humping the anti-tank rifle. It was his baby and only he could give it the love and affection needed to keep it clean and happy, ready to gurgle out a burp of instant death.

But was this Symes?

There was no deformity. His shoulders were square. In astonishment I stared at Hutch, then at Sergeant-Major Heaynes and again at Symes. It was too much. He could not bear it. His mouth split open in a great wide toothy grin and then we were all grinning.

Hutch Burt had fixed it. He had taken Symes to a local tailor who had craftily sewn a pad into the battle-dress shoulder to hide the deformity.

"You be careful Symes", I warned him, "or next thing you'll know is that Mr Burt will have you fitted with falsies out front."

They had surprised me. I was happy, they were happy. We all went off to drink beer with the tank squadron commander. By the time we left him, he was happy.

Back at Winchester we heard the news. No. 4 Commando had acquired two tanks on loan. We could play with them. Commandos who had first enlisted in the Armoured Corps became irrepressible instructors. Beyond the perimeter of Winchester our enthusiasm knew no bounds, driving, pulling levers and traversing the guns. Fortunately, no one supplied us with ammunition, but the knowledge gained was invaluable.

Another experience loomed up. With Murdoch McDougall, I was sent on a course on house-to-house street-fighting in a bomb-shattered area of Battersea. The commandant, a major, showed us round and put us through our paces on the assault course.

He was short of instructors, so he would make a bargain. If Mac and I would help him as instructors, we would get passes to London, the "Hundred Club" and the "Bagatelle". We both tried to look as if we were not too keen on the idea. Then I heard Mac's throaty chuckle, "Oh well! What is there to lose?"

The derelict shells of buildings were the result of air raids on London. Trainees doubled along empty streets, over debris and in and out of ruined houses. Some obstacles were heart-stopping.

Three storeys up a wooden batten spanned the gap from one house to another. You paid your money and took your choice; some ran across, others crawled, some went deathly pale. Below there was no safety net.

At a gable-end window two storeys up I pulled on a line and hauled in a rope. I held the end of the rope, and climbed up onto the window-sill. The calculated difference between two, three or four storeys is immaterial.

All I had to do now, was to screech as if Tarzan, swing out like a pendulum over the abyss and go through the open window opposite, to which the other end of the rope was attached at the lintel.

I pushed off, down and up, and went through feet first. I let go of the rope before it dragged me back. The major had warned me, "Watch it, or you'll damage your spine on the sill edge."

Grovelling on the floor I saw the rope disappear as if an Indian fakir was doing a trick. Big Mac would be coming next, all six foot three and a special size in army boots. Why save a spine only to suffer instant death from McDougall's boots. I scrambled hastily to one side.

Mac hurtled through. Floor-boards rattled and squealed in protest. The building shook, plaster flaked off the walls, filling the room with dusty stour. He got up, scratched the soft down at the side of his head and adjusted his spectacles. He groaned, "Very interesting—but I don't like it much!"

With the trainees, we went to the railway sheds. A green monster puffed smoke and hissed steam. Engine brass and paint-work sparkled, beezed-up on parade. This was for us. We had never played with a Hornby this size and we showed our enthusiasm. The driver was alarmed for this was his own special toy. God help us if we put our dirty fingers on his magnificent engine. Only a few of us at one time would be allowed on the footplate.

He was small, neatly dressed in overalls and had his hair plastered down, smoothly gleaming as if oiled by the rag in his hand. We were no longer hard-eyed, tough, stony-hearted soldiers. We were soon climbing all over the green engine goddess, driving it, reversing it, and worthy of a cartoon by Giles in the *Daily Express*.

The driver looked sad. We all looked sad. Big Mac had just asked a question.

"How do you blow this thing up?"

Sitting down to early breakfast I heard the crump of the explosion. That was a "big one" and it had landed on Winchester. The telephone jangled. It was for me. Sergeant-Major Heaynes reported, "A bomb has been dropped in town and demolished buildings—thought we might be able to help. I am collecting the troop, and will take them there."

I clipped on the web belt and grabbed my green beret. Breakfast would have to wait.

The troop and A.R.P. wardens were feverishly pulling aside rubble and searching for victims. Amid the pile of stone and wood, a great void yawned in the floor revealing the dark murky depths of the foundations. Surely no one would be down there? But people at war in Britain had their own way of beating Hitler's bombers. They constructed air-raid shelters in odd places to which they adjourned, clasping flasks of tea and cross-word puzzles.

Heaynes dropped me through using a trapeze artist's inter-locking grip on the wrists. The drop was deeper than I thought. As my soles touched solid, I collapsed softly like a spent parachute, the way I had been trained. The musky smell tickled my nostrils as I shone the torch into dark subterranean alleys of surprising headroom. There were no bodies, dead or alive.

Heaynes reached down to haul me up. He was slim, medium height, smooth-faced with sparse sandy hair on top. His wrists and arms had a sinewy strength. As I scrambled out Sergeant Woodward lent a hand.

Two or three grey-haired older women had brewed tea from their meagre rations. They tottered around doling it out. As I dusted off grime, I watched big sexy commandos at work, giving the women hugs and kisses. For crissake, who did they think they were? Sheiks of Araby?

"Thanks mum! You're beautiful."

"Hows about you and me going dancing?"

Female hands fluttered to tiny wisps of grey hair and eyelashes trembled. One pointed to me.

"What about that poor man?"

"That's not a poor man, luv, that's an officer."

I gritted my teeth. They would change their tune if I ordered a fourteen-mile speed march. I would have to go too. If I did not, they would start the march and finish the march, but what they would do in between would remain a mystery to the Flying Squad.

Up my sleeve, I had a trump card, an ace, in the form of Lieutenant Hutchison Burt, the son of red-haired Burts. He had a long-playing record of experience in the Brigade of Guards.

Hutch explained his scheme. Aghast, I muttered, "My God, Hutch, it's dastardly."

At Winchester a small tributary of the River Itchen runs fast and deep under a low-arched bridge near to the school's playing-fields. Between the surface of the water and the stone of the bridge there was just enough air space for a human head.

One at a time they went into the river using the flow and keeping balance, feet briefly touching the moving, pebbly mass below. Rifles were held clear, to be fit and clean to use at the other end. Then came near tragedy. A poor swimmer lost his footing and went under the swift current. Instinctively, he held on to his rifle. Quick, instant action saved disaster. Hutch and two others plunged in, grabbed hold of the drowning man and hauled him to the grassy bank, where he quickly recovered.

Heroics and tragedy were forgotten as Lieutenant Hutchison Burt stood up ramrod straight looking like a human sponge, his battle dress sodden and his boots squelching. Red hair dripped and red moustache drooped, ignominiously. Then came the roar that had quelled every flicker of an eyelash on the barrack square at Caterham.

"Get - out - of - my - sight!"

Lovat was made brigadier of No. 1 Special Service Brigade, and Robert Dawson took over command. Dawson was a keen and experienced climber, so long fingernails and extra toes might come in handy.

Sure enough, we went off to St Ives in Cornwall to carry out a rough-weather landing on the cliffs, three hundred terrifying feet, pock-marked by overhangs, chimneys, that mountaineers dream about but which give me nightmares. The code-name for the exercise was "Brandyballs".

At the first attempt, despite meticulous and careful safety precautions, two men were drowned when a landing-craft overturned. We were launched on Royal Engineers' collapsible canvas pontoons from the yawning mouth of a tank landing-craft, which brought us from St Ives, by sea, to face the cliffs at the Brandys. The Navy and local fishermen thought we were crazy and had hastily hidden their boats and their oars.

Kneeling in our flimsy, flat-bottomed barges we paddled in a twelve-foot swell, the way Treasure Island natives handled their canoes. Close in to the rock shelves we let go a kedge anchor at the stern, paying out a line as we tossed up and down, till our bow was at a ledge. The linesman then held the rope taut, allowing the craft to rise and fall inches from the smooth rock slab. Each time the pontoon rose level to the shelf, one man jumped off.

We saw the barge strike the rock, rise up crazily and overturn. Almost at once we were ordered back to the tank landing-craft with the others, while a rescue operation was immediately carried out. Good swimmers stationed at ledges held out hands, threw ropes and jumped into the heaving water, oblivious of danger and with but one single thought—to save their companions.

Nobby Clark of the Mortar Section was a hundred feet up on a ledge in the face of the precipice. He jumped off, hit the cruel sea and broke an arm, but still had the presence of mind to throw his good arm around a drowning man and hold him floating till they were both picked up. Those of us who were waved away now steered towards the bow of the tank landing-craft, standing off, ramp open, as if a great whale was ready to swallow us.

It had been fairly easy to get out. It did not look so easy to get in, bobbing up and down. The parent craft was dipping too, waves foaming and frothing in anger about the ramp, showing displeasure at the attempt to escape its clutches. We went in on the crest, surf riding. As we were swept inboard we tumbled over the gunwales, arms, legs and muscles straining to carry the canvas coracle on to dry metal, before the sea snatched us back.

We faced fact again. Heroic effort had failed to save two men. When the pontoon overturned they had been snagged underneath.

Each and every man was a volunteer in special service. All accepted the risks, the challenges of nature as well as war. There was a cloud of sadness, but no despondency. We buttoned up our lips and emotions while we waited for tomorrow. Lined up on a parade we were given the opportunity to take one pace back. No one moved, no one batted an eyelid and no one twitched a muscle. We all thought we could do it and if we were going to do the landing again, we would do it as we were, together.

And together we did it, the colonel, like General Wolfe at Quebec, leading us to land and scale the Heights of Abraham, but they were called the Brandys.

Some of the high-ranking spectators declined to come forward to the cliff-edge viewpoint. Vertigo is not a pleasant sickness, I did not blame them.

David Haig-Thomas and some of C Troop had become stranded on a ledge from which there seemed no route to climb up. David was not only a first-class climber, but had also explored and lived among the Eskimos in Greenland. For a time he was content to seek sea food and edible vegetation but, as darkness fell, he and his group became impatient. There could be no rescue operation until daylight.

With Sergeant Lindley, David began to search for ways and means of getting up the precipice, the others following. No one wanted to stay on the ledge all night to be whipped by the cold wind and showered by the salt spume, besides, they were hungry. They reached the top in blackness and sped off to join us at supper.

On the following morning, we went with them to see their feat of daring. We hardly dared look, there seemed no possible route up that nerve-chilling, sheer, glossy cliff. But David and his men had climbed it in the dark—ignorance had been bliss!

This part of the coast was lightly defended. We had proved that what seemed impossible, was possible for a highly trained, determined force and, in proving it to others, we had proved it to ourselves.

We had proved that not only did we have a will—we had a way!

## 15

# Royal Salmon—Canadian Capers

Huddled in a corner of the bar, they brooded over me—Portman, Maybury, Carlisle, Heaynes, Woodward and Houldsworth. Brows furrowed in deep thought, they stared unseeing into their pint pots, patiently explaining to me. To be a member of the commando fraternity, you have to be a bastard.

It was not the sort of word I normally used. It did not sound quite right as an endearment for the Superintendent of branches of the Royal Bank of Scotland. So far I had never used it while addressing the branch manager, nor to any of the great bank's customers, not even to those who had been overdrawn a couple of bob.

"Of course", they went on, "there are many kinds, like 'orrible, stinking, lousy, rough, tough, rotten, mean, dirty, crumby, sexy, weak-kneed, bad and not-such-a-bad bastard."

These N.C.O.s were thinkers, philosophers, like the scholars here at Winchester who were known as Wykehamists. With them I could have a course in further education.

Once I had listened in to their discussion on religion. Their knowledge ranged from Tibet to the high Andes, missing nothing in between. What they would not know about the army pay manual and King's Regulations could be expressed on a micro-dot.

I was ignorant. If I wanted to get on and be admitted to the fraternity, I would have to consult the sages, treat them with respect and pay them their dues. The weary barman saw my nod and started refilling. Now I could speak, ask my question.

"What happens if I become every kind of a bastard?"

They stared at me in awe. Obviously I had potential. Houldsworth's broad accent cut through the smoke haze shatteringly, "Eh! But we've got a right one 'ere."

Jock McCall was helping me to pack. Hutch Burt had recommended him to me. Jock was small, burly, a blue-jowled, tough Glaswegian. With the unit we were going to Braemar to go through the Snow Mountain Warfare Course in the Cairngorms. For Jock and me, it was back to Bonnie Scotland, to the hills and purple heather.

The chief instructors were Frank Smythe, who had mountaineered in the Himalayas and had written books on the subject, and John Hunt, later to become Lord Hunt, and famous for his exploits on Everest.

Two days of each week were spent in Braemar replenishing stores. For the other five days, troops went out to separate hill-camp bases from which to assault the high peaks.

Daily we went off in column, loaded like Sherpas, bent under the weight of filled rucksacks, with hands in pockets to practise balance. Already we had practised over stepping-stones and fallen rock. Soon we would be as nimble as mountain goats.

We were allowed to eat on the march and we carried in our pockets strong black chocolate, cheese, biscuits and dried fruit. We must never allow our energy to run down.

The rate of climbing was measured at about 1,000 feet in an hour. Ten minutes after each start, we paused, took off sweat rags and wind-cheaters, divested ourselves of sweaters, then replaced wind-cheaters and sweat rags. When we stopped to rest, the process was reversed to replace sweaters. That way we would not sweat and we would not get chilled. Although the month was June, the peaks were white-capped, and snow and ice filled crevasses and deep furrowed gullies.

Sharpshooters with rifles and telescopic sights were sent off to hide at a distance. They fired near enough to miss us while we tried to follow the ricochet of the bullets and take a back bearing on the furrows made, to spot the marksman.

In the evening, we returned to the hill camp to brew tea and cook jugged hare if a scouting party had been successful, or trout guddled out of an ice-cold river. As the gloaming turned the hills, heather and bracken into purple, deep blue, and gold, the camp fell silent in awe.

In pairs, we crawled into double-skinned tents. A composite ration box placed on edge served as a cupboard and table between sleeping-bags. A primus stove already lit gave light and warmth. The menu would be discussed, the meal cooked and a small piece of pemmican added to the stew to create flavour and add heat to a tired body.

Fresh clean mountain air and a full belly was our recipe for sleep. I was glad about the sleep. Energy had returned to my muscles. I would need all I had stored.

Three thousand feet up, we stared over the edge of the mountain. Scree made of loose boulders, rock and rounded stones was scattered on the hillside as if an avalanche had been petrified.

The instructor had us lined up. We would go, eight at a time, on a scree-run. He bawled. We jumped over, digging heels into the lava-like river, and the mountain became active. Our action had started a wave of pebbly rock. We ran on the crest, ski-ing on army boots, turning at speed as if *Alpini*, arms out-thrown, gliding from one side to the other, exhilarated. Three hours it had taken to climb this mountain and only a few minutes to get down.

Line after line of commandos followed at intervals. Then, all of a sudden, we froze and shouted a warning, "Rock, rock."

A huge boulder had become dislodged and was following the path of a man on his downward run. He looked over his shoulder and coolly moved over to his right. The boulder, not to be out-done, followed. The man looked again, this time in horror. He tried going left, but the massive projectile was bent on his destruction. With a final desperate effort he threw himself to one side, rolling and tumbling on the scree, to curl up on a grassy bank.

Eyes dilated, we watched helplessly. The boulder missed him by inches, bounding, pounding and crushing to reach a green slope and stop by a rivulet. Relief changed horror to derisive yells. The man who had narrowly escaped death was standing up shaking his fist, his curses echoing along the Lairig Ghru.

The Lairig Ghru is a long, long glen. Today it was smiling

enigmatically like the Mona Lisa, a beautiful painting—but what lay beyond?

Two soldiers returning home on leave had elected to take a short cut. They had got off the train at Kingussie and had set out on foot through the glen to Braemar. They had been caught in a snowy hell, a blinding icy blizzard of drifting white. Freezing and exhausted, they died.

We listened to the instructor.

"Climbing and mountains are as sailing and the sea, you've got to know the ropes. Keep a weather eye open and check clothes, equipment, food, dry twigs and matches. You may have to die fighting, so give yourselves a chance to live. The mountains, like the sea, can be smooth or rough, today the mountains are smooth, tomorrow . . . ?"

We hoped that tomorrow would never come.

Jock was pleased for me, but I was sorry to leave E Troop. Hutch Burt would take over troop command. I was the newly appointed adjutant of the commando.

Most of the arrangements for the return to Winchester had been made. I would have to ensure that these were neatly executed. For the occasion I donned my tartan, put a lift to my step, a swagger to the kilt and made the sporran dance to "Scotland the Brave". I thought to put on a show, cutting a dash.

Inside the hotel, I drew up shocked, stunned, gay whistle throttled, brave show by Hie'lan laddie evaporated. The terrazzo floor of the hall was covered with fish, red-brown, gold-flecked, gleaming fish—salmon.

My mind boggled. Fish came from a river. There had been no rain recently so they could not have swum here by themselves and died. The nearest river was the Royal Dee. Royal Salmon? Circumstantial evidence! My knees wobbled. My head would adorn a spike on the Canongate in Edinburgh.

Who would have the cunning, the daring, to commit such an outrage? Who would have the operational experience, the knowledge of ambush, to cut off one end of the river road, then the other, and blow-up what was in between? Everyone in this unit was capable of that. Knowing is not evidence. There must be some way to pin these bomb-happy, fish-fingered merchants.

I licked my dry lips. I could be the first adjutant in the world to put a whole unit, the colonel, officers, warrant officers and N.C.O.s on a B.252 charge sheet. The judge advocate's staff would work overtime. The War Office might have to build an extension to the "glasshouse" to accommodate four hundred extra customers.

We were about to leave Braemar. No one would be anxious to get feet wet, boots dirty and socks soggy. They would have no time to dry out. So? They would take off all their clothes, underpants and all. As explosions heaved the waters of the Dee and fish floated to the surface, men on the river bank would go in to collect the harvest . But naked? My God! It would be a terrible sight.

Furtively I glanced around. No one had seen me and I had seen no one. Fish? What fish? I had seen no fish. There were no fish. Head up, I picked my way through the scaly mass, ran upstairs, sidled into my office and closed the door.

Nervously scheming, I doodled on the blotting pad. A rap at the door made me jump and twitch. McCall entered, banged his feet and saluted. Before he could open his mouth, I yelped, "You. Tell the R.S.M. to get busy. I want this place cleaned up, now, this instant, and", I added darkly, "all evidence that we have been here must be removed."

McCall was quick. He did not take time to salute. I sighed. If I could not beat them, I would have to join them and end up in a hell ship or a salt mine.

The engine-driver blew the whistle and the train rolled. The scene of the devilish crime was fast disappearing. I was settling myself in a corner seat when the compartment door slid back and a disembodied head came through. It was Jock McCall. He leaned forward confidentially and whispered, "Don't worry, sir, the lads have fixed it. They've sent it on to your mother in Paisley all nicely wrapped up in moss and paper, she'll enjoy a bit of fish."

He withdrew, a conspiratorial finger along his nose. The compartment door closed without a creak.

A silver-haired mother would have no suspicion that she was about to become a receiver of stolen goods. Jock McCall had visited her. He had gone up top in the charts along with Lovat, Churchill, Fred Perry, and the Scottish Rugby fifteen. She thought these nice boys in the commando mothered me but look what they had done. They had made *me* an accessory after the fact.

We had hardly time to get our second wind when another exercise was proposed. We would train in the thickly wooded countryside at Brandon, in Suffolk. In the first orienteering exercise, I was told that I would have to look after a very special guest, Admiral Cowan.

Why me? I had a vision of a crusty mariner, scrambled eggs on his cap, one eye and a squawking parrot. I was not keen to walk the plank. I did not like sharks with big, beautiful, well-brushed teeth.

He was small, chunky, loosely built and wore a battle dress with webbing equipment. A revolver stuck out of a low-slung holster. Although he was well over retirement age, nearer seventy than sixty, he was determined to die with his boots on. He certainly kept them well-polished for the event.

Somehow he had got into the action at Tobruk. When Rommel's Panzers overran the town, the Admiral had stood out, alone, firing his revolver at the tanks. With his last bullet gone he had thrown his revolver at them in disgust. He tried to escape, but the crew of a tank chased and caught him. They admired his gallantry and courage. But the Germans were stupid, they repatriated him because of his age. I saw the commando flash at his shoulder. I was glad I did not lose him and glad he did not lose me. I stuck to him like a limpet.

The exercise over, I could breathe, sit in my office and check the pens and inkwells. My jaw dropped as I listened to the colonel's instructions.

"Ronald Menday and I have been called to a meeting in London. I've promised to carry out an exercise with the Canadian tank regiment in harbour nearby. You lay it on," he ordered, "perhaps I'll be back in time to take part."

We took the role of enemy paratroopers under orders to attack and destroy the tanks and crews. Dusk fell and the troops departed, one by one, to their objectives. We saw the star of a Very pistol. The alarm had been raised. Noises travel fast and loud in darkness, the whine of starter motors, the grumble of engines, the roar of heavy vehicles injected with fuel.

There was one piece of information the colonel had withheld, and it was vital. The Canadians had been on survival exercises for over ten days, never being allowed to rest in peace, their sleep disturbed as soon as heads hit pillows. Tempers frayed, nerves stretched to breaking point, the Canadians came out hell-bent, hell for leather. Armoured vehicles, tanks and bren carriers loomed up, milling and threshing like maddened wounded animals in a bull ring.

Some of us, ghostly figures flitting purposefully in blackness, were caught in the maelstrom of ironclads spurning the earth, churning dead wood as crews lashed motors. So this was the Calgary stampede. Tigers climb trees. We went up snarling.

Hutch Burt and E Troop had penetrated the Canadian lines. The Canadians did not stop to dress. They came out pyjama-clad, some naked—all had their bayonets fixed. Undaunted by the ghastly sight, E Troop drew their entrenching tool handles to use them as cudgels. A battle commenced. A real old-fashioned Wild West brawl, a punch-up. When the battle was over, several of both sides were rushed to hospital where broken bones, bruises and split heads received attention.

A report had to be made. Head in hands, I wondered had it been an exercise, a battle or an international incident? Would Honourable Members in the House of Commons ask questions?

Robert entered. I stood up. Unbelievably he was rubbing his hands and smiling.

"Excellent, excellent!"

He had arrived back in time to take part in the exercise. He had managed to crawl under the Canadian commander's command wagon. He had listened in to the battle. He chuckled.

"I could have blown their headquarters' staff sky-high."

"But", I interjected, "what about the troops? I've heard that they might be confined to camp, not allowed to go into town, in case the war continues in the streets and pubs of Brandon."

"Nonsense," Robert waved away the idea. "The Canadian colonel and I talked on the telephone this morning. We are both agreed, there is no need for that."

In the pubs of Brandon that evening, Canadians and commandos met, beer flowed and there was laughter and song. It was voted the best exercise ever. That's funny, I thought, British and Canadians think alike. Before making friends, they have to knock the living daylights out of each other. After that comes the hugging and head patting.

I had seen the Canadians before. They had made the main effort at Dieppe. They had met murderous gunfire with courage, gallantry and determination. With their numbers decimated, they had fought on to the bitter end. They had treated the Germans like a great big Calgary steak. They had taken one helluva bite—a taste of what was to come.

# 16

# A General of the Royal Marines

When, I asked myself, am I going to get leave, see the sight of London, and the sleepy-eyed dolls. The colonel was full of ideas, but not mine.

The commando was to be split up into two halves, one half at a time going to the Norfolk Broads for special training on small craft. Blakes Holidays Afloat, a cabin cruiser, skipper's cap and a few wavy rings on my sleeve might give adrenalin a boost. These navy chaps had a girl in every port. On the Norfolk Broads, one port would not be far away from another. Dawson and Menday were a problem, nattering about boat training and underwater swimming using reeds. I did not want to be a broken reed.

We went into a tented camp a few miles from Wroxham. Each day we went off to handle small craft, cabin cruisers, speed-boats, and became human submarines breathing through periscopic reeds.

Robert told me that Lovat was coming to visit him and he would bring a guest, the commanding officer of No. 1 Special Service Group, General Sturges of the Royal Marines. Lovat wanted to talk to Robert Dawson in private, and what better place than a remote camp in Norfolk. I was ordered to arrange an exercise to entertain the General, something he would enjoy.

Sub-sections were lined up, ready to go. They had to race to Wroxham, where there was a bridge over the river, to craft collected for them. They were not to cross the river by the bridge, but swim across using reeds if they had to. They could then take the boats, make a course for Wroxham Broad, land, and speed back to camp by map and compass.

As they went off, the General and I scrambled for the staff car waiting with its engine ticking over. We arrived at Wroxham, boarded a speed-boat, and were ready to see the fun. We watched as troops pulled themselves out of the river and over gunwales to jab starting motors into action.

I set the speed-boat going, the bow rising proudly cutting a wake in the water. McCall and Maund, acting as orderlies, were happily seated at the stern. The boat race began.

At the Broad, a craft similar to the one I piloted, came up on starboard, making across our bow. The General was up, grey hair flying in the breeze, ruddy face irate and blue eyes blazing.

"You bloody fool! You'll miss the inner berth."

Galvanized into instant, desperate action, I shoved the gear lever forward and the craft responded. We swept along neck and neck with the other boat to the hard. Out of the corner of my eye, I saw the General stagger and fall back at the sudden thrust of power injected into the engine. On the other beam the impudent helmsman was wavering. I gunned the engine recklessly and held a course to cut him out.

The quay was coming up fast. There were no disc brakes on this thing. I hauled on the stick, paused in neutral, and rammed it into reverse. The boat stood on its beam ends, lashing about like a hooked porpoise ready for the gaff. As the rocking craft subsided in the foaming water I turned and went rigid in horror.

The General had recovered from a near backward somersault. The reverse action, hard astern, had now propelled him forward, hands first, about to take a dive. He managed to grasp the gunwale and stop, head over the port side, where he could see his own distorted features reflected in the water. And then—then his cap, with the red band and gold braid, slowly began to slide from his grey hair and topple into the water.

Stupefied, mesmerized, I watched him make a last despairing effort. Leaning out precariously, he stretched an arm and caught his cap as neatly as a first slip playing for England.

Water lapped at the side of the boats, exhausts purred, engines cut and throttled. The crews were in neutral.

He clambered ashore, put on his cap and pulled down the long service-dress jacket. When he came about, we saw a general—an angry, indignant, hot-tempered, red-faced general . . . a general of the Royal Marines.

His language flowed in a torrent like Victoria Falls, a great flood drowning me in an ocean of curses. A terrifying education worthy of honours at Plymouth. Breathless at last, he turned off the tap and growled, "Let's get on with it."

The exercise finished, I cleaned up and changed in my tent. Jock was quietly sympathetic. Thrawn, bolshie and rebellious, I snarled, "What the hell's going on here? Who wanted the inner berth anyway? I've a good mind to tell him to stuff the . . ."

Jock's eyes were flickering. His head jerked to the V-opening in the tent. Framed in the triangle was a nice, pink, grey-haired, good-natured face. The eyes were kindly, creating an image of my favourite, understanding, generous uncle. My mouth fell open. The General was smiling.

"I am going down to the village to post a letter, I thought you might like to come, we'll take the car and send it back with the driver. You and I can have a pint and a stroll back."

Over the rim of the tankard his eyes sparkled with amusement. He was insisting, "You Scots are a dour, thrawn and bloody-minded race."

"Yes sir," I agreed. "At Murrayfield or Hampden Park, at play or in battle, we are never defeated; we only suffer slight reverses, like the ancient Scottish chief called the 'Bucktoothed'."

"Who the hell was he?"

This was the cue I needed.

"The 'Bucktoothed' was given that name because of the two prominent teeth which protruded over his underlip. When Vikings raided in the North, their leader met the Scot in hand-to-hand conflict, a desperate struggle. The Viking killed the Scot, cut off his head as a trophy, and tied the grisly prize to the saddle bow on his steed."

I paused to let the picture sink in, then went on.

"As the Viking rode from the field to return to his homeland victorious, the head of the 'Bucktoothed' bumped against his leg and the protruding teeth penetrated the Norseman's thigh, causing a wound. By the time the Viking reached his homeland fjord and the deep bass sound of the welcoming horns, he was dead. He died of a septicaemia."

The General was chuckling hugely.

"Some story! I might tell that to the Marines."

"No sir, not that story. Tell them I haven't got buck teeth, but they're good. No need to knock my block off."

He laughed quietly all the way back to camp.

Climb chalk cliffs? The colonel must be crazy, and I had only just recovered from the shock of a proposed operation at Cap Gris Nez.

Brian Mullen had dreamt up the scheme. His idea was to use an aircraft at night to go low over the French coast, releasing several 100-foot lengths of rope with hooks attached, to provide ready made cliff-climbing ladders for commandos. The ropes would be fastened to the tail plane of the aircraft to flow behind, like streamers, while flight cones would be used to make the ropes fly straight in the slipstream.

With other little diversions by the Royal Air Force to keep German heads tucked under blankets, the Mullen special operation might go unnoticed. Off shore, commandos in assault craft would be stealthily creeping in to land on the tide, with motor-torpedo boats of the Royal Navy close in attendance to lend a hand. It would require only one out of ten rope hooks to snag in the wire defences on top of the precipice, and allow a strand of hemp line to dangle to the beach. Commandos in rope-soled shoes would not need a second invitation.

Brian needed help to perfect his equipment for the operations. He collared Jed Price, his pal, small, sharp-faced and a humorist.

"What about using piano wire?"

Jed Price was an electrical contractor before the war and had a friend, a top class engineer in Birmingham. If Brian Mullen and he could get leave to go there, he was sure something could be done. The Colonel showed interest. I groaned inwardly.

Price knocked at the door. His engineer friend answered and waved Mullen and Price into the house. He listened as they explained their urgent need. Mullen drew sketches and plans to illustrate the gadget. In forty-eight hours, all was complete and handed over, without question.

Plans for the operation could now be discussed and put forward for consideration. These captured the imagination of Combined Operations Staff. The operation was never carried out as by this time the resources of ships, aircraft and men were being stretched and priorities were strict. The Mullen adventure went "pending possible".

Here I was, at the troop leaders' conference, about to listen to another dicey blind date.

The commando had moved to Seaford in Sussex by the sea, excellent for a holiday. I needed one. Encounters with "top brass" had put my nerves through a mincer.

Nearby at Burling Gap, white chalk cliffs rose up eighty or ninety feet high, or, from a bird's-eye view, eighty or ninety feet down. Crumbly cheddar cheese, that a mouse could pick holes in, and we had Big Mac wearing the McDougall tartan and an outsize in army boots.

We would get help. No safety net, but a rope. That was thoughtful. Also, the colonel had dreamed up a gadget. So that was the thing that was cluttering the table.

It was a light-weight equilateral triangle, each side measuring two feet, with a pulley wheel at the apex and a roller at the base. The metal was about two inches deep and, along the bottom edge, it was slotted into shoes which, when pressed into the soil, held the contraption immovable, the way shoe spikes steady golfers.

The Colonel explained the dicey bit first, keeping the spicy bit for "afters". We were asked to presume that a small group, paratroopers or members of the Resistance movement, had got to the rendezvous, at the top of the cliff, with a rope and a metal "Dawson".

When we landed, the group at the top of the cliff would place the triangle, the apex with the pulley wheel at the edge. They would then lower the nylon climbing rope over the roller and pulley wheel.

The first man below would tie a bowline round his waist, lean well back and take the strain, put one foot on the cliff face, and signal by giving a tug on the line. Up top, the group would haul steadily, human donkey-engines, walking inland, away from the precipice. Then what? The man below, a spider on a thread, would walk up the cliff. Ingenious! But would it work?

He was adamant. We would try the new lifting apparatus, the "Dawson". As usual, we practised and practised until he was pleased, then he ordered a full-scale dress rehearsal.

Dressed in field service marching order, the commando embarked on assault landing-craft at Newhaven along the coast. We sailed out to sea and made the run-in, line abreast. The ramps went down. We dashed off, splashing in the shallows, going helter-skelter up the beach. Some carried extra "Dawsons".

I saw a man tie the line. He leaned back, put one foot on the cliff face and tugged on the end of the rope. Then he walked up the sheer white, chilling, chalk cliff. Another and another, and as more men reached the top, more gadgets were put into use. Soon we were all up, some 400 men of No. 4 Commando, in just under thirty minutes. We had done some stunts before, but this beat everything in Billy Smart's circus. But for a raiding operation?

Commando-type operations were based on meticulous planning, high speed, physical endeavour, overcoming elements and natural obstacles, with determination and a will to win.

More was needed. In a commando, men accepted cold

calculated risks. They were prepared to gamble with their lives. They were young, life was precious. That was O.K., but they valued chances where they themselves could show their paces, reduce the odds, become the favourites for selling their lives dearly.

But who could expect a group of men to be at the right map reference on an outlandish cliff top in enemy occupied territory, at the exact time, on a given night, and to co-ordinate with a landing operation from the sea, relying on time, tide and phases of the moon?

Phases of the moon affected some people. A gang of people I knew had run about naked blowing salmon out of a royal river in Scotland. When normal, they liked a dark moonless night, for dark daring deeds.

Brian Mullen made a suggestion. His was a fertile, creative brain.

"How about trying out a harpoon gun to shoot the line? The fish-hook might catch in the wire or hold on the ground. If we managed to get one man up, we'd all get up. The weight of the harpoon gun is no problem and the noise when fired could easily resemble a beach mine erupting."

The idea was considered and stored, but not forgotten. Boffins scratched their heads and information was passed around. Perhaps these pirates in the Special Boat Section of combined operations would find it suitable. They were "nutty" enough to try anything and small raids were their pride and joy. Someone might find the "Dawson" useful—and someone did.

At the Pointe du Hoc in Normandy, scraggy, rocky, earthy cliffs rear up. The precipice claws like a sickle to cut the skyline. Here, in the invasion, the 2nd Battalion, the United States Rangers, landed in a hail-storm of bullets fired in enfilade from each side of the hook. The bay inside became a devil's hellish brew of death. The screams of the dying were not yet of pain, but of men still screaming for victory. Americans like to win, they want to win, "Gee man! We don't go for losers."

Decimated, they fought on. They came from Texas, New York and the Bronx, from Chicago and from the streets of San Francisco. They were here, they were there, they were everywhere, thumbing the hammers of their Colts, Garands and Bazookas.

They had climbing ropes and "Dawson" triangles. A few

scrambled to the cliff top. With the metal triangles the spine-chilling deadly assault speeded up, nylon line running smoothly on the pulley wheel. They wanted some fast goddamned action and they got it.

At the Pointe du Hoc, a simple stone obelisk marks the spot, a moonspace of craters, the deep impressions of exploded shells. The green grass cannot hide, will not hide, the desperate wounds. The cliff drops sheer while its sickle hook embraces a sandy beach, a curling arm protecting the saga of those who had dared and those who fell on the beach, by the seaside.

Standing on top of the cliff, by the memorial, memories flow as fast as the rushing tide. The sound of voices, the commands, cries and curses, the din of battle. Tortured courage and gallantry in array—the United States Rangers.

## 17

# The Brotherhood of Man

A military genius had removed all the road signs. This made it more difficult for the Germans if they landed in Britain. There were no posts pointing to London, Glasgow, or even Llanarmon Dyffryn Ceiriog. So how could I get to Llanarmon Dyffryn Ceiriog without asking?

Maps were issued, Ordnance Surveys of an area, printed in colour on linen texture. These show roads, rivers, railways, church towers and spires, the contours of hills and a host of other details. A study could give a sense of direction. Some have a natural bent for map reading, others learn the hard way.

Lieutenant Veasey commanded a section in A Troop who were expert with explosives. He was known for some reason as "Fiji" and was large, dark-haired and brown-eyed with a sense of humour.

With his section, he had been on a map reading and compass march. At a road junction there had been an argument. Fiji won. "This way," he insisted. Finally, after a few extra miles on unwilling, tender feet, they arrived at troop headquarters and were dismissed. At once they made a bee-line for the pub, to cool off. Fiji pushed open the door. Breathlessly, he offered his apologies.

"O.K. boys! The drinks are on me."

No one moved. Great hulking backs showed an iron curtain.

"Come on chaps, let me buy you a pint."

The bar was stilled, never a movement, the cold war was declared. Anxiously, fearfully, Fiji made his big appeal, "Aw! Come on fellows, speak to Fiji."

Deathly silence followed. They were skulking and conferring but suddenly, the scrum broke up, grinning.

"Yep! O.K." They would drink with Lieutenant Veasey.

Some time later, Fiji checked his watch. He had better get going. He was due back at his billet and he was hungry. He gave his excuse, said, "Cheerio chaps," thrust out into sunlight and fresh air, and mounted his bicycle parked at the kerb. Hands firmly on the handlebar grips, one foot on the pedal, nicely balanced, he pushed off and spun the chain. Explosions like Guy Fawkes crackers repeated in quick succession. The cycle collapsed in the gutter, Fiji too. Astonished, he looked up mortified. At the pub window, row upon row of bright, happy, mischievous faces shone like neon lights. Raised beer mugs cast reflections. Lovable, tender, sweating feet had been avenged.

After the retreat of the British Expeditionary Force from Dunkirk, Winston Churchill had asked the Chiefs of Staff for "bands of brothers" to take the fight to the enemy. He got them. Commandos, a brotherhood of man, up to all the tricks.

After an exercise, Fiji discovered that while his pack had been loaded with bricks, his section had carried empty cardboard boxes.

"Alright," he muttered to his sergeant, "Next time, I will check the weight."

They were lined up for inspection. Fiji tested each pack carried at the shoulder blades. He could not lift them. Off they went on the exercise to return grinning happily. Fiji was suspicious. He found out that they had only empty cardboard boxes in their packs. They had cunningly tied string to the buckles at the bottom of the pack, laced the string underneath their armpits and tied it to the buckles on their equipment braces hidden by ammunition pouch-brassières. Fiji gnashed his teeth. By God! Next time he would take nothing for granted. He would look in every pack.

When they were ready, Fiji checked that there were bricks in every pack. Success was his. He did not check his own pack as his batman had filled it and it was heavy.

The exercise finished, Fiji was pleased. "O.K. chaps, well done, you can throw away the bricks now. We'll do a speed march, run and walk, back to Troon and the Bridges Bar."

His section hastily got rid of the bricks and formed up eager to go. Fiji was howling for his batman. "Hey you, get these bricks out of my pack."

"But you haven't got bricks in *your* pack, sir."

Fiji's jaw dropped. "What do you mean, no bricks in my pack? If I'm not carrying bricks, what am I carrying?"

"Well sir! There's your landlady's iron, the head of her coal-hammer, some of her cutlery, your razor and a pair of your best shoes, all neatly packed in cardboard boxes and softened by a few pairs of your army socks."

The section sergeant cut in.

"Permission to move off, sir?"

Distracted, Fiji nodded and turned back to his batman. He was too late. His batman had joined the section which was moving off at the double march with boots bashing a rhythmic beat on the tarmac. Fiji started to plod heavily behind them, his shouts and curses drowned by his section's age old cockney cry . . . "Any old iron, any old iron".

We were sorry when Fiji left to go into action with another unit in Italy. Word came back that he had been captured, but had jumped the train taking him and others to a prison camp in Germany. He had escaped and shown initiative and cunning by not immediately playing his hand. Instead, he lay up in a culvert till the hue and cry died down and then found his way to Switzerland. He had no map, but his training had taught him something. His wits had been sharpened and he knew how to find his way around.

Commando raids kept the Germans jittery. Small reconnaissance raids brought vital information. If we missed the boat we still had a duty to get back and, therefore, an escape kit was issued. In it were some foreign banknotes and maps drawn on rice paper which could be eaten. On my battle dress, I had one button, like all the others sewn on, except that this one was a compass. If I balanced it on the pin stuck in the seam of a lapel, I could get a rough north, south, east and west. And every "Cub" knows that the stars and vegetation help direction by night and by day.

Pat Porteous was keen on small-boat training and his Troop, D Troop, were labelled the boating troop. Every spare moment was spent at Newquay, in Cornwall. They favoured a dory, a small type of high-prowed, fishing boat suitable for landing in surf. At the right moment each man went over the gunwales to haul, keeping up the momentum of the waves, to beach the craft, before the tide sucked it back.

When a small reconnaissance raid was proposed before D-Day, it was given to Pat. He chose a few of his specialists, along with his inseparable companion, Lieutenant Mike Burness.

An M.L. (motor launch), skippered and crewed by the Royal Navy, took up station two or three miles from the enemy-occupied coast of France. The dory, carried on davits at the stern, was dropped into the sea with the raiders aboard. Using the Austin diesel engine, they surged towards the shore. Closer to the beach, with the engine shut off, muscular arms pulled oars set in muffled rowlocks. A hushed, soundless trip.

The tiny force landed. Leaving one man to mind the boat, they began their task of surveying the beach and land defences. They wormed their way towards a pillbox. It was undefended.

Balked of their prey, they set off along the shore track. At a suitable place they sank to the ground, moulding themselves into the contours. The trap was baited. They hoped that German sentries on tour of duty might walk into the ambush. They were unlucky. No one appeared.

Returning to the boat, Mike Burness touched off a beach mine and was slightly wounded. The others helped him to the waiting craft, pushed off, and taking a back-bearing on the compass, made the rendezvous with the M.L. returning to England with vital information. Perhaps next time they would bring back several different varieties of Heinz.

Peter King, the dental sergeant, who had lost rank when he had stolen a boat to make a personal raid on France, never lost his enthusiasm. Later, at Walcheren, in Holland, he and a signaller, O'Donnell, who had been badly wounded on D-Day, crossed the sea in a collapsible rubber dinghy to land, in darkness, on the German occupied island of Schouen. They stole up to a ruined building. Upstairs, at a gable-end window, they had a perfect observation post.

From there, they sent back by radio, to No. 4 Commando, a

constant stream of information on German activity on Schouen, regularly changing to pre-arranged frequencies to avoid discovery.

The commando did not know that Schouen would be bypassed and the Germans isolated to be mopped-up later. Inactivity is demoralizing. Such little operations provided more than information; increased morale and experience.

I had gone out twice as a spare officer on a small raid, when half the commando, 200 men, under command of Major Menday, sailed from Dover in two landing-craft infantry. The object was the destruction of a V-bomb site in Holland.

Well on our way, we ran into phosphorescence. A strange occurrence, perhaps caused by a myriad of fish. A ring of bright water encircled us, advertising our presence like cruise ships in festive mood. We were unable to shake it off and, with the element of surprise gone, we returned to Dover.

Time, tide and phases of the moon governed the dates on which the operation could be carried out. It was early February. We had to wait a fortnight.

At the bow, dressed in thick woollen duffle coats, my group huddled together for warmth against the cold wind and salt sea spray. A man cuddled an anti-tank rifle. Its armour-piercing shell could shatter a searchlight or puncture the thin hull of any German E-boat daring to thwart our mission. We were only four miles from enemy-held coast, when suddenly, brilliant cones of light beamed from the shore. Searchlights criss-crossed, the sea sparkled with reflections. Our craft veered off to seek the shadows and lie still.

Slowly the searchlights converged to spotlight a ship stationed off our landing area. Peals of deep thunder followed red-orange flashes as German coastal gun-batteries spewed shells. Fascinated, we watched. The Germans were battering a target ship, practising night gunnery. If we had been half an hour earlier, or had the Germans started their exercise half an hour later, we would have been the target for tonight. That's life!

Dedicated commando, Captain Charles Trepel, disappeared with his tiny force of Frenchmen on a small raid in the winter of 1943. What happened? No one knows. Some ships—like some aircraft, did not return.

The wind taken out of our sails, we returned once more to Dover, to mount the operation again. It was never carried out.

Every available ship was being harboured in a pool which would break its banks. We would sail on a flood tide of Allied might. At dawn, a host of gallant ships would break the white ensign to flare out a challenge, echoed in the thunderous roll of guns and the mighty roar of the cruel sea. Commandos would storm the beaches on D-Day, and my skin would crawl to the ranting, raving, scream of the pipes, "Come ye sons of dogs—and—we—will—give—you—flesh!"

In the end . . . when we landed
. . . there was light . . .
a burning flame

# 18

# Raggle Taggle—Wild Csardas

It was 1944 and summer.

No. 4 Commando had returned to Britain to re-group and re-equip. Other operations would be planned for them. I could only hope that my tour of duty at the Commando Basic Training Centre would allow me to rejoin the unit in time.

The Ivanhoe Hotel in Buchanan Street, Glasgow, was unchanged. So was the waiter serving hot tea and toast at the hangman's hour.

Earlier, when I had been an instructor at the C.B.T.C., a tall, lanky American Ranger had drawled, "I gotta tell you guys yo're gonna have t'button up yore flies, button up yore lips an' button up yore combat suits—yo're gonna have t'git out there, and do—somehow—somewheres . . . yo're gonna have t'die!"

That Yank sure spilt a bibful. I felt like death as I staggered across to Queen Street Station where the train for Spean Bridge left from Platform 9. It was 0500 hours on a cheerless morning.

I had put on my MacLachlan tartan and stuck a *sgian-dhu* in my stocking. I had nothing to fear from Lochiel and Camerons in Lochaber.

A MacLachlan of Corounan had been standard-bearer to Lochiel on the fatal field of Culloden. MacLachlans were intermarried with the Cummings of Achdalieu who held hereditary right of burial in the Lochiel enclosure, conferred on them by Sir Ewen Cameron of Lochiel. Not that I wanted to claim the right at the moment. I had had enough of slit trenches, but I could be driven to make a claim if Jock McCall started to play the bagpipes. In a weak moment I had agreed.

Then there was that "Red Coat", the commandant of the Commando Basic Training Centre, Lieutenant-Colonel Charles Edward Vaughan. During Vaughan's occupation, the castle had been set on fire, a forest had blazed, salmon had been blown up out of the Arkaig in front of Lochiel's nose and a favourite rhododendron tree had been hacked to pieces by an enthusiastic Frenchman trying out a machete. It was high time a MacLachlan was back at Achnacarry to keep an eye on Vaughan.

The train eased out of the station, wheels squealing on the curves and chattering over the points. It began its rhythmic drumming and I settled down to look out of the window, ready to view the colour slides.

I saw Clydebank and Dumbarton with great ships held by the stocks. Huge cranes towered above as sleek grey shapes of destroyers slipped up and down the Clyde. Merchantmen plied to and fro, splitting up from convoy, or hastening to join the flock of craft carrying the lifeline of supplies.

Helensburgh, Rhu and Bowling, the playgrounds of amateur yachtsmen who had had professional dedication. They would be skippers of cruisers, destroyers, motor-torpedo boats and minesweepers in this war.

On I went to Crianlarich, bleak Rannoch Moor, Tyndrum and Bridge of Orchy, past high hills and long deep glens with white foaming torrents gushing down craggy rock ravines, to Spean Bridge.

I got down from the train, saw Jock McCall and waved. He was already at the luggage van. Only a few others alighted, a few locals and some soldiers returning from leave. The soldiers would catch the truck to Achnacarry and I would do the same. But he was here, at the station, the Colonel, in person. Was it possible that he had come to meet me? Ben Nevis winced as I stamped my feet and came to attention in salute.

"'ow are you, Donald?" He was smiling and proffering the hand of friendship.

Cautiously, I took it, glanced over my shoulder checking arrivals on the platform. Insidiously, using the name of his greatest favourite, I asked him, "Expecting somebody? Lord Louis? Royalty perhaps?"

He gave his hoarse rumbling chuckle. "Good 'eavens," he gasped, "you know very well you'd get lost without me to take you by the hand."

In the hotel, Mrs Macdonell served us with coffee. She was godmother to all commando soldiers seeking the comfort of a fire, a soft seat and a belly-tightening meal.

"Amazing!" I exclaimed. "Here I am just back from battles,

bombs, bullets, billets and bawls, and all they can say to me up here is 'och! it's yoursel-eff'."

The Humber staff car purred smoothly away and crossed the River Spean to take the hill on the Inverness road to the junction at the top. Wilson, the driver, took the left fork and slowed at the bend on the road where the Mucomir Falls tumble, fizzing and gurgling over rocks into the broad expanse of the River Spean. A quiet peaceful place where a man could fish, dreaming his own dreams, with the reel running softly and the line whispering through the air, to drop the fly on the shimmering water as sweetly as a kiss.

Farm buildings clustered together on a hillock. A Cameron who owned it was famous for his strength. He was known far and wide simply as "Mucomir". Vaughan was listening.

"Mucomir was a great character. He could toss the caber and throw the hammer. One evening, a friend visited him in a pony and trap, a two-wheeled carriage. After a small dram, Mucomir came out of the house with his friend, to put his feet on the road and they saw that the pony had pulled the trap off the hard shingle and into the peat bog, and no amount of hauling, coaxing or cursing could get the pony to pull the vehicle out. Finally, Mucomir flexed his muscles, bent his knees, and grasped the shafts of the trap where they protruded at the back. Then expelling compressed air, a weight-lifter blowing energy, he up and lifted the carriage from the peat bog, on to the hard stony path.

"Mucomir straightened his back. Surprised, in a soft Highland voice, he spoke, 'Pwhell! pwhell! No wonder the puir horse couldn't pull it out, I could hartly lift it out mysel-eff.' "

Moments later we were over the lock gates at Gairlochy and on the twisting switch-back road to Achnacarry.

With the Colonel I stood on the forecourt of the C.B.T.C. and let the sounds seep in—the constant rattle of machine-guns, thump and crump of explosives. Nearby, the water of the Arkaig frolicked over rounded stones, laughing at man's inhumanity to man.

A soldier was negotiating the overhang on the battlement of the castle to abseil down a perpendicular wall. C.Q.M.S. I. Frickleton and I had devised that one. The idea was that a man could lower himself on a rope from the top of a building, to imitate a spider on a strand of web and swing from side to side, chucking hand-grenades through windows.

Vaughan jerked his head. He growled, "My God! You and Frickleton gave me a lot of trouble with that."

"Oh! Why?"

"One of the trainees was a bit over-enthusiastic, swinging about. He missed the wall and went right through the officers' Mess window. I 'ad an 'elluva job getting it cleared up before Lochiel saw it."

There were changes in the Officers' Mess. Dickie Hooper had operated in Yugoslavia, Spud Murphy in Norway and Johnnie Proctor had been on the St Nazaire raid where he had been severely wounded and lost a leg. He had been discharged and had gone back to a job in civvy street. But, with all his friends still serving in a commando, the work he had to do irked him. He had applied to get back into Special Service, and had been accepted.

At the end of each course, Vaughan spoke to trainees. "You will go to a commando, perhaps you will go on a raid. You may be wounded, lose a leg or an arm. But remember, there will always be a job for you, up 'ere, at Achnacarry!"

Big deal. Who would want to come back here, minus a limb? John showed me his tin leg and proudly pointed to the autographs on the metal, inscribed at an Officers' Mess party.

My bed was made up with army blankets on top of hard-packed palliasse sections called "biscuits". As Rabbie Burns, the Ayrshire poet had pointed out "better a wee bush than nae bield". Compared with a wee bush and a slit trench, I had four-poster luxury, the four posts in this case being the legs raising the bed from the bare floor, and I would only be here for three to six months.

Life was not dull. The "banshee", for instance. That caused an uproar.

The permanent staff at Achnacarry were physically fit. What with the weather, the hills and marching about at the double, it was nothing for them to be up and away with the "leave truck" to Fort William.

One man had dallied overlong with his girl friend. At the Town Hall he was late and the truck for Achnacarry had gone. The Colonel had explained the distance and his attitude.

"It's only eighteen miles, 'owl for transport and I'll pin your ears back!"

But eighteen miles on dancing commando feet! These were his

treasures to be exercised gently by a wee waggle here and a wee waggle there and told stories of the little piggies that went to market. Eighteen miles is a long, long way for ten little piggies.

He returned to his girl friend. Yes, there was a bicycle and he could borrow it. Luckily it was not raining, although it was dark and fast approaching the midnight hour. There were no lights on the bicycle. The pale streak of moonlight was enough. Who would be out at this time of night in Lochaber?

Bah! Of course he was not frightened. Banshees? A lot of old wives' tales. These damned Scots were always telling a lot of daft stories. Banshees! He chuckled and showed his teeth.

Suddenly, before him, an apparition emerged from the ground, a disembodied face and two hands. Instinctively he applied the brake and wobbled precariously. A cold shiver ran down his spine and the hair at the nape of his neck prickled. Then he hit the grass verge, lost control and crashed head over heels into the soft bracken.

Gasping, he peered upwards. Was this a banshee? It spoke.

"In the name of the law, cycling without lights on a public highway."

When the summons arrived at Achnacarry, Vaughan growled, "This whole thing is ridiculous."

"Oh no, sir! You can't say that. The constable was showing dedication to duty. That soldier might have been an enemy agent. You have issued operational instructions for use in an emergency. Within minutes the Commando Basic Training Centre, staff, trainees and all, could be mobilized into a fighting force and you are well-known far and wide as 'Rommel of the North'. Why shouldn't Hitler have a go at you and try to disrupt the training of commandos at Achnacarry. You know we all work hard up here to win the war."

He looked suspicious, but gradually his face softened. He liked the idea that he was a thorn in Hitler's flesh.

Events followed fast. Robert Dawson, Len Coulson and Big Mac had written requesting my return to the unit. The war was not yet finished.

Then V.E. Day arrived. Charles Vaughan was to be de-mobilized. I could not go back to my commando without pulling off his army boots.

Lunch was very special. Afterwards, we trooped out to the

forecourt of the castle, where Wilson, Vaughan's driver, stood by the Humber staff car. Matson, the Mess sergeant, brought drinks—a wee doch-an-doris. All the officers gathered round for the toast, "Slainte."

I nodded at Pipe-Major MacLaughlan. He blew the reeds and the notes skirled and danced to the "Skye Boat Song". The tune changed and we were hushed at the sadness of the pibroch, "Will ye no' come back again".

At last I saw him to his car. The roof was pulled back so that he could stand up and take what was coming to him. I got in front beside Wilson, and four dispatch riders took the cue and kicked the starters of their motor cycles ready to lead as escort.

Charles Vaughan was not royal, nor a prince, but in his way up from the ranks he had acquired royal and princely ways at Achnacarry. This was Scotland, Glenfinnan was not far away—and his name was Charles.

To the sound of three cheers and the brag of the pipes, we set off down the tree-lined avenue, to slow at the gates. The guard turned out to present arms. As the car turned left on to the road, out of the hillside every commando and trainee rose from the bracken and heather to cheer and cheer. Cap-comforters and green berets were doffed to the wartime Laird of Achnacarry.

At the bridge over the Spean, locals gathered to wave and wish him good luck. If he was no' a Cameron, he was almost as good!

Like Lochiel himself, Vaughan had made history in Lochaber. A host of soldiers of many nations would speak of him with awe and pride, with the name "Achnacarry".

I could not have him bursting into tears at Kingussie Station. I fussed around. "Watch you don't catch cold. Put that tartan rug over your knees."

For the first time in his life he had no reply. He was not crying . . . but then, he was not laughing.

I fingered the letter in my hand.

Captain Albert McVean wanted me to be the best man at his wedding. He had been in my Company in the 9th Battalion, The Cameronians (Scottish Rifles). He was one of three well-known brothers, all of whom served in the same regiment.

Earlier he had been posted to the King's African Rifles in Abyssinia, where he was probably in hot water exchanging unfriendly smiles with the poor crocodiles. He had made his request. From 4,139 miles away, I could reply nonchalantly, "Sure, pal, I'll see you turn up, shaved, washed and properly dressed, on time."

As soon as the newly wedded couple left on their honeymoon, I departed for Germany, but before crossing the Channel, I stopped off in London to get engaged to Anne. She had red hair and brown eyes. I had met her at a party at the Café Royal.

With all these French, Belgians, Dutch and Americans about, I had kept her locked-up in the strongroom of my wallet, where the perfume of Christian Dior and Helena Rubenstein wafted a fragrance to overcome the normal fusty smell of moth killer guarding a faded ten-shilling note. If there were to be any combined operations, I would handle them as top secret, for my eyes only.

With Jock McCall I disembarked and checked in with the R.T.O. He sounded like a travel agent anxious to please.

"Things are a bit tricky at the moment and you might have to wait a day or so. But Yvan Peten of the Belgian Troop of No. 10 Inter-Allied Commando is here. He is going home to Brussels and he has a jeep. Why not go with him? Have forty-eight hours leave. I'll fix it with No. 4 Commando."

I stared. Was he Thomas Cook, or the son?

Yvan Peten was a compact bundle of energy, dark-eyed and curly-haired. He could fit the star part in a Hollywood movie for a swordsman. On the way to Brussels he took us via the beautiful old city of Bruges. As we approached a junction at the end of a narrow street, I saw the gendarme at the opposite pavement. Then came the crash. The huge lumbering red truck hit the jeep, bouncing it to cannon into the gendarme, sending him head over heels into a shop doorway. McCall was at my side. "Are you O.K. sir?"

I turned from the jeweller's shop window. Somehow I had been thrown out of the vehicle and had staggered over to look at the diamonds. Also I was worried about the policeman.

A café proprietress fixed us up with black coffee and smeared red soapy disinfectant on my cuts and bruises. Yvan and McCall had escaped injury. The jeep was still in one piece, the engine willing, but the body weak. When the gendarme had been sent off to hospital, we took a train to Brussels and went to Yvan's parents at the Avenue Lester Plissart, to recover, before going on to Germany.

On the outskirts of Recklinghausen, Jock and I fell silent. Allied bombing had left little standing and the town had been reduced to rubble. Railway engine sheds were a shattered mass of twisted girders. Engines and wagons lay thrown as if a model train-set tossed aside by a spoilt child. If there was a front in this war, civilians were in it. A bitter eye for an eye, a tooth for a tooth. If the rest of Germany was like Recklinghausen, the Germans would have no teeth left.

The Colonel was pleased to see me. Len Coulson and Big Mac closed in, and I moved my feet before they were crushed to pulp.

There were changes. Some members of other commandos had been posted to No. 4 to replace those lost in action, ill, posted elsewhere or demobilized. The main duty was to guard a camp for very important prisoners but the troop I took over had special tasks.

We had to carry out house raids to seek out arms and explosives stored by Nazi sympathizers. There was also the problem of displaced persons now roaming the countryside, seeking revenge by killing German farmers, and stealing.

We went out on night patrol in jeeps, at high speed, switching off the lights and engine to coast silently by hedgerows to come to a halt and listen. No one thought it odd that we were now protecting Germans. British soldiers do not go in for murder. They represent the best in law and order and they have sharp, shrewd, legal army minds.

"You're joking, Kennett. You! Sergeant-Major of the Signals Troop, nearly court-martialled?"

"No sir, I'm not joking. It was a near thing. The signals officer, Peter Beckett and three others, wanted to go the officers' club in Brussels. Captain Beckett asked me, 'Alright if I take the jeep?' I agreed, 'Sure! As long as you bring it back. I'm responsible for it.'

"When the four officers came out of their club in Brussels, the jeep was gone. They were horrified. They searched without success. It had been stolen and they had a problem. They solved it. One jeep looks much like another, except for the regimental and unit signs painted on them. The officers picked a good one, got it started, and returned to Recklinghausen. I took one look at it, muttered 'Christ,' then started praying. Some of the lads gathered round. They chortled and drove it away. The following day they brought it back with all the regimental signs changed. To outward appearances, the jeep belonged to No. 4 Commando.

"So I relaxed and all might have been well, but the same four officers went back to Brussels, two weeks later, in the same jeep.

This time they made sure it wouldn't be stolen, and it wasn't. A 'Redcap', a military policeman, was guarding it.

"'Good evening, gentlemen, is this your jeep?'

"'Oh yes,' the officers chorused, 'that is our jeep.'

"'Ah! well now, gentlemen, can you explain why the engine number is the same as the one reported stolen two weeks ago? We've been searching for it ever since.'

"That started the investigation and since the jeep was in my charge, court-martial proceedings were taken against me. Supposing they bust me to the rank of private and ordered me to pay the cost of the jeep. At a soldier's basic rate of pay, two shillings a day, I'd be as old as Methuselah before I squared the account.

"The officers told me not to worry. An operation was being planned. Meanwhile evidence was gathered into the military government offices. I worried. It seemed as if I was doomed. But shortly before the date for the trial a huge party was held in No. 4 Commando Officers' Mess, to which all the officials and staff of the military government were invited.

"As you know, we have in the unit an expert cat-burglar and we have masterminds who don't leave much to chance. They knew the building, the room and the filing cabinet to be 'sprung'. They were going into this thing like a bunch of Chicago mobsters about to 'heist' a bank.

"As darkness fell, and the party reached its height of merriment, the cat-burglar shinned up a drain-pipe and entered the building, found the room, the filing cabinet and the dossier on the case of the 'Jeepers Creepers'.

"The file disappeared and red-faced military government officials disappeared. With no file, they had no case. I was reprimanded by the C.O. who barely kept a straight face. I had difficulty too.

"You see, sir, when you take on one member of No. 4 Commando, you take on the lot, the whole unit. It was a close shave, but then, with this lot, I'm used to close shaves all the time!"

My troop sergeant was McNeill, a Scot, another Glaswegian. He wore on his green beret the black hackle of No. 9 Commando.

We went up the steps of the billet, a block of flats. In the hall a German youth was rummaging. McNeill touched his shoulder and the lout looked up, surprised. He ducked low and dived for the exit showing a large bottom. McNeill's boot sent the scavenger flying through the air, the way Andy Irvine scores between the posts for Scotland. "Don't steal from McNeill!"

Although the war in Europe was over, there was still the war in the Far East, and there were other problems. The colonel, Robert Dawson, had solved one.

Those due for demobilization were impatiently waiting for the day when they would go home to civvy street, their wives and families. They would have to re-adjust, re-train, and re-orientate. Robert had thought it necessary to help in the transitionary period from soldier to civilian and had started a scheme.

Employment courses had been started in engineering, mechanics and driving heavy vehicles. Local breweries and factories were being used for work experience. Big Mac was running a course in languages.

At the time of enrolment, the man applying for a course stated the type of job he preferred, and the town or area in Britain where he would like to be employed. The colonel sent his own staff car and driver back to Britain with Captain Peter King. King was sent details of each man under employment training and the town selected. Peter travelled up and down Great Britain arranging jobs.

When a soldier was demobbed from No. 4 Commando, if he wished, he had already trained for employment and knew the name and address of his employers.

Non-fraternization was an order. This took away from the troops their social life. There was no canteen. Instead there was the risk of undercover night life in some dark, dismal, sleazy joint. Was there an alternative? If so, what was it?

I turned to that tough Glaswegian with the black hackle on his beret, Sergeant-Major McNeill. I put it to him. I growled, "I don't want my troop to go marching backwards and forwards to meals carrying knife, fork, and spoon in the neat little pockets made for that purpose in the battledress. Get somewhere. Get tables, chairs, table covers and proper ashtrays. Get local help in the kitchen, and someone to scrub the floor."

Empty premises nearby were requisitioned where there was space, a good kitchen and a bar counter. It may have been a restaurant at one time. It was certainly going to be one soon.

A corporal was put in charge. He had the ideas of a Reo Stakis.

Scrubbing began and the kitchen was made spotless. A German painter was employed to re-decorate. When all was ready for inspection, McNeill took me round. There were tables, chairs, table-cloths, real ashtrays, and cutlery was set at each place. The Reo Stakis fan was not satisfied. "The walls are a bit bare. We could do with some pictures."

If I did not think up something quickly they would be off to Paris to loot the Louvre. "Perhaps you can find an artist to do a few murals. There's plenty of space between the picture rail and the cornice."

The corporal produced the artist and he produced his own personal copy of David Wright's *Ladies out of Uniform*. The artist transferred the ladies from the magazine onto the walls.

A bar was started for beer and wine only as no spirts would be allowed. The bar would open at the evening meal and then only for those off duty. Young Germans were employed as waiters. The troop would be allowed to entertain a limited number of guests from other troops.

Financial accounts were posted every week on the notice-board. Profits were made and a dividend paid out in free rations of chocolate and cigarettes. Occasionally an extra bonus was declared and cash set aside for those going on leave. There was just one small niggling worry—what would happen when they took over Krupps, I. G. Farben and all the local breweries?

Now that the Troop was settled, I could take a night off. With Len Coulson, Big Mac and a few others, I went to the officers' club in Recklinghausen.

We played a game called "Cardinal sin". A champagne bucket was filled with beer and a measure of gin for each officer present at the table, was added. When the bucket was passed round, I could drink or not, as I pleased. As the concoction was drained, the game became intense. If I failed to finish the contents and allowed the officer next to me to do so, I would have to pay for all the drink. Conversation flowed.

"I used to play the violin. I've played a duet with Jean Rennie of the Scottish Orchestra."

Seven pairs of eyes stared.

"It's true. She wasn't in the Scottish Orchestra then. We were both children. Although she was asked to play a solo, they didn't ask me."

Len Coulson spoke. "You never told us before that you could play the violin." He waved towards the German orchestra. "You could play your party piece now."

I shook my head. "Good Heavens, no! Not here. Once I might

have had the nerve. But not now. I read a book once by Walter Starkie. This chap made a journey alone in 1929 through Hungary and Roumania, carrying only a rucksack and a violin. He fiddled his way among gypsies. Like him, I fancied drinking Palinka, a brandy, and playing wild csardas."

Len Coulson was not to be put off. "How about playing a wild Scottish csardas right now?"

"Come on, Donald, show these Germans how to play a Scottish reel or something."

"Let's have Loch Lomond."

They pushed me to my feet. There was no escape. I had not played a violin since I was 12 years old. Strong hands guided me toward the maestro with the violin.

He listened obsequiously to my request. Dismay and horror spread over his features. Maybe his violin was a Stradivarius.

I half turned and pointed to the seven commando officers. Seven pairs of cold, bleak eyes were focussed on the Germans. The orchestra had jerked their heads to follow my pointed finger as if I had served an ace down the line on the Centre Court at Wimbledon. They jerked their heads back to the maestro, making an appeal. Seven commando officers were seven more than they would like to take on and Big Mac was glowering, not a happy picture for a pin-up.

I played a bar at a time, the orchestra following with improvisations. Not bad. We had another rehearsal. We were ready, the club members hushed and expectant.

With a flourish of the bow, I gave them the cue and the wild Scottish csardas concerto began. I played it cunningly, very quietly, letting the orchestra do the work and drown my sound. It was not bad. I returned to my table, after exchanging bows with the orchestra leader, amid deafening applause, and to a standing ovation from my companions.

Flushed with success, I asked them, "Should I do an encore, something else?" Firm hands pressed me down to the chair and held me there. Big Mac's hoarse chuckle came across.

"My God! Enough is enough!"

# 19

# Lenzil "the Ghost" and Van Nahuijs

Len Coulson and Big Mac offered to take me on a guided tour of Flushing (Vlissingen), the scene of the night assault landing of No. 4 Commando. The operation, code-name "Infatuate", was a direct frontal attack against a heavily defended town. I thought about it and I was appalled, remembering the raid on Dieppe and the terrible losses suffered by the Canadians. I could have nightmares, although the casualties borne by No. 4 had been slight at Flushing. But why?

At Dieppe, Canadian courage and determination had not been enough to save them from catastrophe. The Dieppe operation had been a raid in force, there had been no follow-up, no intention to stay or create a second front. The Flushing action was different in this respect.

Although only part of a general attack mounted on Walcheren by an Infantry Brigade and a Commando Brigade Group, the assault was a test of the sound training, nerve and confidence of every soldier in the relatively small commando force. It suited their role, needing leadership, initiative, dash, and experience to overcome obstacles, with swift surprise, operating in the dark. But a direct assault, bang on to the mole in Flushing Harbour? It seemed an impossible feat against long odds.

Before going to Flushing, I collected small pieces of information. It had become a habit. If I could fit in the small pieces of the jigsaw puzzle I would get a picture. Len and Mac would add the colour, the laughs, the sorrow and the blood.

The Germans had occupied Walcheren in 1940 and fortified it strongly. It was part of the "Atlantic Wall", their defensive system.

After the Normandy landings, the Allies needed the harbour of Antwerp to unload supplies, the guns and butter for troops along the lines of communication. German guns on Walcheren covered the Scheldt, preventing any ships from entering or leaving the Belgian port. Drastic action was needed to give a lifeline to the forces of liberation.

Zeeland consists mainly of three strips of land, like the fingers of a right hand, pointing westward to the North Sea. The middle finger is South Beveland and Walcheren. Although Walcheren is called an island, it is in fact a peninsula, linked by land to South Beveland. The connection was formed when the channel between the two, Het Slot, was filled in, reclaiming 1,200 acres of new land.

The tip of Walcheren Island is shaped like a saucer, with dunes and dykes facing the outer rim. It lies at mean tide level. When the tide is high, the land is below sea level, when low, it is above. Breaking the saucer's rim would let the ocean in. The Allies bombed the dykes to wash the Germans out. The flooding, with the ebb and flow of tides, brought swift currents sweeping away the top soil and leaving salt brine in its place.

The people are not unlike the Scots, with whom, long ago, they carried on a trade in barter. They are a religious people. In South Beveland, there is a distinction between Protestant and Catholic women. Protestants wear a rich white lace head-dress shaped like a conch shell, while the Catholic bonnet is a trapezium through which a light blue under-bonnet can be seen.

Under the heel of the Nazis, the Dutch were joined together in prayer for liberation. Their reclaimed ground, hard won from the sea, had been blown apart by the bombing of the dykes to further the Allied war effort. Food was scarce and many had to subsist on flower bulbs. When boiled these were edible, but had an over-sweet cloying taste. Luckily, the Dutch had a good supply of Worcester Sauce which disguised the sickly flavour.

They had suffered stoically as they had suffered before. Their colouring is darker than those in more Northern provinces owing to the Spanish occupation which came to an end about the time of the Reformation around 1572.

Their resistance movement was active, Van Delft told me. He managed a shipyard at Flushing. When the Germans arrived they had seen a ship's keel laid down. They ordered that the vessel should be completed at once and the Dutch, with families at risk, were forced to obey. By the end of the war, some five years later, the ship was still on the stocks, uncompleted. The Dutch had worked on it, but things seemed to go wrong. Steel plate meant for Flushing ended up back where it came from, consignments of parts never arrived, machinery failed to work. Yet, as soon as the war in Europe ended, the ship was speedily finished—but for Holland.

Colonel Robert Dawson still led the commando. Major Bill

Boucher-Myers had returned to the unit to replace Ronald Menday now a colonel in No. 2 S.S. Brigade, Italy.

Major Bill Boucher-Myers had been second in command of No. 4 Commando back in Winchester. Some time before D-Day, he had been sent to Staff College. Bill was a regular soldier. He had been with the commando on the Lofoten and Dieppe raids but here was the chance to advance his career, and further, to gain valuable experience which would be available to the unit. He did not get back in time to sail in the Armada of 6 June. But now he had returned. The Colonel, Robert Dawson, had kept a place for him. Bill Boucher-Myers had arrived when all his experience, training, operational and administrative, could be used to the full.

Bill was married to a Troon girl, Winifred. He was good at tennis and golf. After the war, he would be elected captain of Old Troon Golf Club, a course which was the result of a twisted, sadistic mind. Now he was involved in the planning for the assault on the town of Flushing and facing up to opposition and defences, the result of minds which were twisted, sadistic and bent on destroying any who sought to drive and wedge their approach to the green sward beyond the concrete bunkers.

The I.O. (Intelligence Officer), Ken Wright, was small, slightly built and bald, with a frill of curls either side over his ears. He was a member of the famous house of Lloyds of London and there could be none better to seek out and assess the marine and other risks. His was a meticulous computer brain.

Philippe Keiffer, Guy Vourch, Alex Lofi, and the French were still firmly attached to No. 4 Commando. Léo Hulot, their Prince Charming, tall, dark and handsome, would survive this war, only to be killed later in French Indo-China.

The Dutch Troop of No. 10 Inter-Allied Commando was also attached. One of their number, a captain, Lenzil, was slim, sallow-faced and dark-haired. After the war, he would become known as "the Ghost". Fighting for his country in the Far East, Lenzil was wounded and left in the field as dead. Later he was picked up and brought into hospital where his leg was amputated. He returned home in time to read his own obituary.

No. 4 had collected a volunteer, Captain P. van Nahuijs, a former police inspector of Flushing. He would not only provide the unit with a great amount of very complete and accurate information about the town of Flushing during the assault planning period, but he had also offered to return to the town with the commando. He was well aware of the consequences to himself if he was captured by the Germans. He was to prove invaluable, leading and guiding the troops in the thick of the battle.

Intelligence work is like editing for Reuters cutting and joining, sifting the material to get simple fact, not fiction. In the Flushing operation, a number of civilians with knowledge of the town were available for questioning. If these civilians were properly interrogated a great deal of information could be extracted both from their personal knowledge and from air photographs displayed to them, and at the same time a check could be made on the citizen's reliability.

There was an erection in Bellamy Park which baffled the photo interpreters as to its possible significance. Civilians were able to say at once that it was a harmless bandstand. These air photographs were very reliable and a most productive source of information. But the importance of being able to read and interpret can hardly be over-emphasized. Pilots of the Royal Air Force had risked their all to get the photographs. These were of more value to junior commanders than maps.

From maps and air photographs, a sand-table model was made. This had to be as accurate as possible. Troops had to be warned that it was only a guide, that when they arrived on the ground the actual shape of churches, houses, yards and contours might not be exactly the same. But the salient points would be there, just as they had been described on a model for the D-Day assault on Ouistreham in Normandy.

Time spent in reconnaissance is seldom wasted and time spent in passing on details of Intelligence reports to each and every man is never wasted. There had to be tight security. All understood— there could be no careless talk.

Towards the end of October 1944, the operation to clear the approaches to the port of Antwerp were still in progress. On the south side of the Scheldt estuary, the Canadians had captured Breskens on 22 October and were driving the Germans westward to the sea. To the north, Walcheren Island was still in enemy hands, though to the east, the island of South Beveland was in the process of being wrested from their grasp.

A plan had been devised to attack Walcheren from the west, south and east, as soon as possible after the capture of Breskens. An infantry division was to force its way along the causeway from

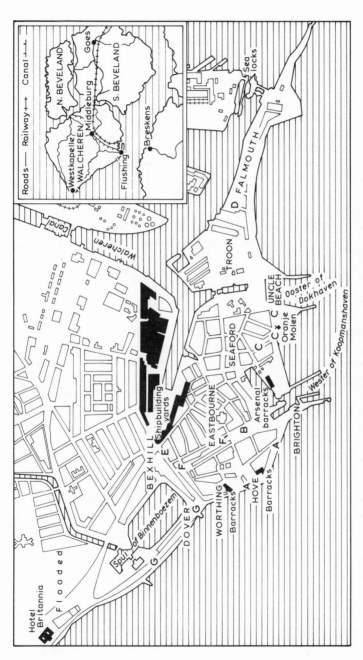

4. Sketch map of Flushing drawn by Under Officer R. M. Cardwell, Ayrshire Army Cadet Force, from records and information supplied by Major B. W. S. Boucher-Myers, DSO, second-in-command of No. 4 Commando for the assault on Flushing. Troop objectives were named after towns in Britain where No. 4 Commando was billeted.

South Beveland, while two forces were to carry out seaborne landings at Flushing and Westkapelle. The landing at Westkapelle was given to a Commando Brigade Group. No. 4 Commando was chosen for the assault on Flushing, followed up by an infantry brigade.

The whole plan of attack was governed by the extent of the floods that resulted from the breaching of the sea walls by the Royal Air Force. By the end of October, the greater part of the island was under water, including the streets of Middleburg and the northern part of Flushing, which, for the assault, was divided into a number of sectors, each given a code-name.

The principal buildings in Flushing were grouped in a sector known as Seaford. From the landward side these could only be approached through the sectors of Bexhill and Dover. The only beach suitable for the assault landing was the pre-war bathing beach in front of the Hotel Britannia which was heavily defended. From the hotel, a raised promenade with the sea on one side and floods to a depth of four feet on the other, led into the town and from the south-east end of the beach a high sea wall ran round to the entrance of Wester of Koopmanshaven. To the east of this small harbour, the sea wall continued to the start of the promontory near the Oranje Molen, a brick-built windmill and a very conspicuous feature on the waterfront. In its length, the sea wall presented a complete obstacle against any assault landing.

From the Oranje Molen a sloping dyke wall ran round the promontory into the small bay called Ooster of Dokhaven, a mud flat at low water. Air photographs showed that the bank at the far end of the bay inclined at an easy angle. But both the bay and the promontory were protected by anti-landing stakes.

Two groynes ran out into the sea on either side of Ooster of Dokhaven, and from the base of the eastern groyne, the dyke wall continued to the extreme tip of the mole at the entrance to the main harbour. At this tip, there was another possible landing beach. But again the only route into the town was very exposed and narrow, this time along the mole itself.

Information about the German garrison of Walcheren was limited. The main battery position and prepared defences were pin-pointed, but the identifications and dispositions of the various enemy units were difficult to ascertain. The final estimated strength of the German garrison was about 9,000 all ranks. Rather less than a third was thought to be in Flushing.

The defences of the town were formidable. The whole waterfront was wired and the dykes and beaches were screened by anti-landing stakes, some with shells fixed to them. There was a system of mutually supporting pillboxes and strong-points, a whole mass of fortified houses, barracks and a bomb-proof tower. All the approaches were covered. Flak emplacements had also been sited so that they could be used in a dual air and ground role. Artillery support was available from batteries located to the north-east and north-west of the town.

The commando still had the two French troops attached. The unit was also given additional sub-units under command or in support—one section of a Dutch troop of No. 10 Inter-Allied Commando, a commando group reconnaissance party, a forward observation officer and a Royal Artillery representative party, one squadron of L.V.T. for stores, one platoon of Royal Engineers from G.H.Q. troops, one landing-craft obstruction clearance unit, a light section of a Canadian field-dressing station, a detachment of naval beach commandos, a detachment of naval beach signals and one section of a pioneer company. Somehow the tough, hard-skinned gentlemen with the calloused hands of the Pioneer Corps had got in on the big act with the commandos.

The commando had taken into its fold an odd collection of happy warriors. The total force of about 550 all ranks would embark on 20 L.C.A.s. This force was now about to take on in battle an enemy totalling approximately six times their number.

The assault was to be supported by five regiments of artillery, three medium regiments and some sections of heavy and super-heavy batteries. Four other medium regiments were available for counter-battery fire.

The most difficult part of the plan was to find a suitable landing site. Information had been received that the bank at the landward end of Ooster of Dokhaven, Uncle Beach, was a dump for rubble and rubbish. For this reason, it was thought likely to provide firm going for vehicles.

Unfortunately, the anti-landing stakes prevented the first flights from going direct to Uncle Beach but it was hoped that the troops would be able to scramble ashore over the dyke walls somewhere in that area. The exact spot could not be chosen in advance.

There were several enemy strong-points in the vicinity. It was believed that these could be rushed and overcome provided the touch-down of the landing-craft followed closely on the lifting of the artillery concentrations.

It was decided that the unit would land in the area of Uncle Beach in three flights at 0545 hours on 1 November 1944.

The unit's objectives had been code-named after towns in which they had been billeted in Britain. A troop honours list— Bexhill, Brighton, Dover, Eastbourne, Falmouth, Hove, Seaford, Troon, Worthing. A small but significant fact.

## 20

# Assault by Night on Vlissingen

The troops gumshoed down to Breskens Harbour at 0315 hours. Part of the harbour was still mined and booby-trapped but one jetty was in use and alongside, the L.C.A.s were moored.

One hour later they were on board. The leading craft slipped its moorings and nosed out into the River Scheldt. Since the weather was unsuitable for heavy bombers, the Royal Artillery took over the job of softening up the enemy. A hellish bombardment started at 0445 hours. Big guns thundered and flashed and fires were soon blazing in the town of Flushing, while craft cruised in darkness keeping an eye open for mines and one-man torpedoes.

Suddenly, the silhouette of the windmill, the Oranje Molen, was thrown into relief against the glare of burning buildings, giving an unmistakable guide to the landing area.

At 0545 hours, the assault began. The first flight closed on the beach as the artillery concentrations lifted. As the leading craft stood into the bay, one L.C.A. moved too far to starboard. It struck some anti-landing stakes, was holed and sank. But the craft with a section of No. 1 Troop edged on to the tip of the promontory and touched down. They scrambled up the dyke wall, cut a gap in the wire and were winkling Germans from their dug-outs before a shot had been fired.

Elsewhere, ramps went down. Commandos stormed ashore swearing frightful oaths as boots encountered underwater obstacles. Huge German naval-type shells were attached to the stakes jutting from the oozing mud. If one big boot connected with a detonator cap, an explosion would follow which would not leave much of the boot, the soldier or the harbour at Flushing.

White tapes were laid forward inland from the gap. A signal light blinked. The way was clear for the second flight to come ashore. Lieutenant Harry Hargreaves, R.N.V.R., and his naval beach party were ready to receive them, and already the Royal Engineers were clearing mines either side of two berths in a garbage tip.

An L.C.P. went out to tell the incoming assault craft that there was room for only two craft to approach the landing place together. At this moment the Germans opened up with red tracer from 20-mm cannon. The fire was high and the second flight landed without casualties, sailing under the flaming arc of red tracer shells.

By this time, the section of No. 1 Troop already ashore, had cleared the promontory of the enemy and captured a 75-mm gun. They were pleased with their new toy. They had learnt to fire German weapons.

As No. 2 Troop doubled along the promontory, they ran up against a dual purpose 20-mm gun emplacement. They assaulted the defence work and captured twenty-five prisoners including the German company commander. They then blitzed along the waterfront from pillbox to pillbox supported by the gun they had seized.

The enemy was now thoroughly aroused. When the third flight came ashore, the Germans opened up with machine-guns and 20-mm cannon but few casualties were suffered. One boat with the heavier equipment for the initial stages of the operation—3-inch mortars, No. 22 sets, and the handcart belonging to the Royal Artillery representative party—hit a stake 20 yards out, and sank in three feet of water.

All the equipment, the 3-inch mortars and radio sets, was salvaged under heavy fire. Commandos and signallers were quick to retrieve these precious items. The signallers swam ashore carrying their R.T. sets. The mortar section scrambled to land with their weapons, all except Knyvet Carr who was in the water slowly going under. They fished him out. He was still lovingly clutching a 3-inch mortar. While Knyvet shook himself like a terrier, his section set up the tubes ready to fire. His command froze them in shocked surprise.

"The section will now clean the mortars, as for cleaning in the dark."

There was nothing else for it but to strip and clean the weapons, firing pins and all. They had them re-assembled and firing within half an hour.

Other troops had already streaked off to their allotted tasks. Someone must have remembered that Big Mac had been in a house-to-house street fighting course. With Sergeant McVeigh and a little group of men, he was in the thick of the battle, weeding out the enemy, dashing madly from building to building over rubble and through shell-holed walls. There had to be quick thinking, fast reaction and cool, deadly accuracy on the trigger.

Tragedy struck F Troop. Private Donkin was over forty years of age, the oldest man in No. 4 Commando, a miner, with a wife and nine children. He was their favourite character. Confronted with a group of Germans, he had stood up, four square, feet apart, and blasted with his machine-gun. The Germans had gone down like ninepins, their faces showing shocked surprise. All but one and he shot Donkin. McVeigh arrived and shot the last German. But for Private Donkin the war was over.

The time was now about 0715 hours and it was just getting light. Meantime, the medium machine-gun section had been led straight to Bexhill by the former police inspector of Flushing, Captain P. van Nahuijs.

A *Flakvierling*, a four-barrelled 20-mm anti-aircraft gun, and a machine-gun post were causing trouble in the Boulevard de Ruyter and Gooseje Busken Straat. These were neutralized by sniping at the crew of the *Flakvierling*, by mortaring the strongpoint and firing Piat bombs at the embrasures.

There had been great activity at Uncle Beach. The landing-craft obstruction clearance unit had cleared the obstacles at record speed under shell fire. Elements of the leading battalion of the infantry brigade follow-up troops landed at 0830 hours. The unloading of stores started and the section of Pioneers rolled up their sleeves and worked with a will to win. A steady stream of German prisoners were being used to keep the beaches clear and to assist the handling of loads over the mud flats.

The Colonel, Robert Dawson, set up his battle headquarters in a shelter near a searchlight post on the Oranje Molen promontory, captured in the initial assault.

The night of 1–2 November passed quietly except for a desperate attempt by the Germans to break through with the help of flame-throwers. This attack was stopped by the marksmanship of the French troops.

The German military and naval commanders had their headquarters near the Hotel Britannia. Their presence must have stimulated the German troops in this area because No. 5 Troop had a hard task to clean up Dover.

The troop started to attack down Goosje Busken Straat. Any attempt to advance in the street itself was out of the question so both sections had to "mousehole" their way through the houses. A small group found an excellent position for its Piat, on the roof of a cinema. Others swung on gutters to reach upper rooms. One man, held by the legs, hung down from a roof and shot his way into an upper storey.

The troop was preparing for the final assault on the pillbox and *Flakvierling* position, when it was ordered to pull back to allow Typhoons to give the Germans a preliminary strafing. The aircraft flew almost parallel to the waterfront to avoid inflicting casualties on commandos and successfully shot up the strong-point.

Continuing their advance, the troop reached the corner house overlooking the strong-point and opposite a building which the enemy still held. The garrison of this building bolted and was mown down by fire. Then, just as a commando was about to dash across to the pillbox entrance with a made up "Pole" charge, a white flag fluttered from a loop-hole. Three officers and fifty-four very shaken Germans were taken prisoner and Dover was at last clear of the enemy.

The first direct assault on the waterfront of a strongly defended port since the raid on Dieppe in August 1942, had been successfully concluded.

By the evening of 3 November, 155 Infantry Brigade with the King's Own Scottish Borderers and Royal Scots had passed through the breach blown in the defences by the combined operation, and had fought their way into Flushing.

Once again, No. 4 Commando had overcome what seemed impossible, taking in their stride a variety of obstacles, and in the dark. They had used the black screen of night and speed to gain surprise. They had used every weapon in their armoury and had fired German weapons as well. Their casualties had been slight, a tribute to efficiency, training, discipline, demeanour, dash, determination and courage—and the meticulous study of correct information!

The military prisoners of war were sharply divided into two categories. Some had no stomach whatsoever for the fight, because they were already suffering from other stomach troubles of a serious nature. One prisoner of war begged to be allowed to retain his patent stomach powder, while another wanted his hair restorer more than anything else. Others showed a total lack of appreciation of realities by insisting on being taken back for their walking-out suits. All said resistance was pointless. Commandos nodded. Walking-out suits for Germans were pointless too!

It was D + 3. The commando boarded L.V.T. These craft ferried them to rejoin No. 4 Special Service Brigade in the Zoutland area. The brigade, consisting of No. 41, 47 and 48 Royal Marine Commandos, had assaulted the beaches at Westkapelle on 1 November, aided by motor-torpedo boats and the battleship H.M.S. *Warspite*. Despite heavy casualties suffered by ships and men, the Royal Marine Commandos had landed to take a firm grip. With them, No. 4 would go on the rampage to eliminate any further resistance by the Germans on Walcheren.

About 0815 hours on 6 November, while a batch of German prisoners was being searched, four Germans were seen walking through the undergrowth nearby. They were at once challenged by the regimental sergeant-major who thought they were part of a fresh batch of prisoners. These men were fully armed. On being interrogated, they stated they had been sent forward by their officer with a view to making a formal surrender of all remaining German troops in the area.

Ken Wright, the Intelligence Officer, and a runner accompanied the Germans back to the Company Headquarters, a dugout situated surprisingly near to No. 4 Commando Headquarters. The German Officer telephoned through to his regimental commander.

The regimental commander, Oberst-Leutnant Veigele was ready to negotiate. He sent a car and Robert Dawson and the Intelligence Officer returned in it to Vrouwenpolder. The order to cease fire had already been given and the artillery bombardment and air strike due to be made on the Vrouwenpolder area at 0900 hours was stopped, cancelled by Robert Dawson.

The local inhabitants were intrigued to see a British officer sitting on the bonnet of the German commander's car. At first they were in some doubt whether or not to wave and cheer. The beaming smile on the Intelligence Officer's face did not leave them long in doubt. There was a lot of waving and "thumbs up" before the car drew up outside the German headquarters.

Oberst-Leutnant Veigele was waiting for the commando party at the head of his regimental staff. They were conducted to his office with great formal courtesy after an elaborate exchange of salutes.

The German commander then made formal surrender of his troops. Speaking with great emotion, tears in his eyes, he declared that the disorganized state of his troops and the lack of ammunition compelled him to take this step. He asked only that his men be treated well as he considered that they deserved good treatment because of the stubborn resistance they had put up under difficult conditions; that his dead might be honourably buried and his wounded well cared for. He was assured on all these matters, and that full honours of war would be granted to the German soldiers.

A total of just over 900 German prisoners of war marched into the commando cage and a number of others surrendered to No. 41 Commando, as a result of orders received from the German regimental headquarters.

The frontal assault on Flushing, a heavily defended town, from the sea, at night, showed that when all branches of British forces were brought together, with leadership, discipline, training and *esprit de corps*, they were invincible.

The motto of Combined Operations is "United We Conquer"— they had conquered.

---

## 21

# Epilogue

The atom bomb blew a spiral of dust, a smoke screen to cut off the heavens in the hope that St Peter and the angels might not see the desolation below. The world was stunned, so were soldiers. With their purpose seemingly gone, all they desired was to go home and start another life while there was yet time. The moment had to be faced.

The Colonel, Robert Dawson, had been demobilized. We had pushed him up on a table to do his party-piece, "*Alouette*", while we bawled the choruses. Puggy Pugh had taken over command of No. 4 Commando.

I had come back to London. There was opportunity to enter a new sphere. VJ Day changed that, and I had married Anne. Jock McCall had returned to the Post Office to take up employment as a driver. He had not told me he had a licence to drive. The inseparable Len Coulson and Big Mac had bought adjacent cottages at Drummore, Wigtownshire.

Colonel Charles Vaughan was keeping a jump ahead. With the help of his close friend, Glasgow businessman, Bill Gilmour-Smith, he had started a Commando Association and Benevolent Fund. Commandos had come through hell together and they were determined that companionship hard won in desperate circumstances should not be lost.

To this day, newsletters are posted from the Commando Association to far-away places all over the world. Old commandos refuse to die, and Charles Vaughan was determined that they should never fade away. To make sure they would not, he picked Henry Brown as Secretary of the Association.

Henry left school at the age of 14 to work in his father's grocery business. He became one of the first Hore-Belisha conscripts and signed on in June 1939—for six months! As a staff sergeant in No. 1 Commando he sailed with them to the Far East, was bombed in the Mediterranean, and arrived at Alexandria in time to celebrate Christmas 1943.

No. 1 was in action in Burma where the fighting was often fluid. The Japs had tried to infiltrate, a flanking movement had been forestalled and the whole of the commando had turned to face the menace. But in the rush to action, they forgot to tell Henry.

Henry had his head down. It seemed just another day in the life of a staff sergeant. He was happy. For once, no one was bothering him with stupid questions.

"For crissake, Henry, are you still here?"

"Of course, you fool. Where do you think I'd be, playing gin rummy with the Japs?"

"Jesus! Henry, no fooling, we've had a helluva battle with the little men. If you were here all that time, you were away out front. Just you pal. What did you say about playing gin rummy?"

It took a long time before Henry could speak. He even stopped typing. It was that serious.

Henry was now typing again giving commandos opportunity to meet, to remember the day, remember the deeds, remember the dead—and not forget the living.

French commandos parade at the Arc de Triomphe in Paris on 28 February each year to perform the ceremony of the flame. It is symbolic. The flame burns every second, every minute, twenty-four hours a day. So, too, it burns in commando blood, a golden link hotly forged in battle—an heirloom to be willed to the sons of the fathers.

At Ranville in Normandy, on 6 June, a commemoration service is held. There, a British cemetery lies side by side with a German cemetery. An Englishman and his wife have joined hands with a German and his wife. Strange, they say, that we each have to lose a son in battle before we become friends!

As Maurice Chauvet, the wolf with a lock in his jaw, often said, "Wa-ar! Ees crazee!"

At lunch in Caen in the School of Domestic Science with Jean and Marie Deschamps, the French couple who had waved to me as I cycled past the *mairie* at Bénouville on D-Day, I asked a burning question.

"Does anyone here know Janie of the Scameroni?"

*"Oui, mais oui."*

The cuff of the empty sleeve of my youthful guide was tucked into his jacket pocket. He was the young boy who had been bringing cattle into safety during the invasion. He had been severely wounded by shrapnel and had lost an arm. Commandos and airborne troops had rushed to his rescue and had speedily sent him to a regimental aid post. He was now working in a bank and taking a course at the university of Caen.

Janie had married the leader of the Free French Resistance Movement in Normandy, Commander Leonard Gille. Janie was irresistible.

The badge of the Scameroni, a winged dagger with the coat of arms of Normandy, has the initials F.F.I., Free Forces of the Interior. A tiny head of a man represents Scameroni, blindfolded for members before D-Day, and for others, receiving it after, the eyes of Scameroni see France free.

I saw the church to which townspeople had rushed during the tank and gun battle for Caen. The crush of humanity squeezed tight, had alarmed the French authorities. They contrived to send a message to "Monty". Despite the destruction to buildings, reduced to rubble all around, the church was undamaged and the congregation unharmed. A tribute to the mercy of God, to "Monty" and the accuracy of British gunnery.

Just along the road from my home at Doonfoot, Ayr, there is a slated, red sandstone bungalow occupied by retired Chief Constable of Ayrshire, Charles Jack and his wife, Kay. It was Kay Jack's brother, Frank Martin, who, at the battle for Caen, volunteered to carry the urgent message to "Monty". Frank Martin got through the enemy lines on a motor cycle. War weaves a web.

Lofi, the black-eyed, burly, bustling Frenchman, was now Officer en Chef aux Equipages, Toulon. In the Mess, a French officer spoke disparagingly of No. 4 Commando. Lofi wasted no time. He dived over the table, picked the fellow up and threw him out of the window. Unfortunately for the poor chap, the window was not open. Now, when Lofi is angry, there is a great shout, "*Ouvrez la fenêtre, s'il vous plaît!*"

Svei Zuit is a broad-backed, heavily bearded Israeli. He is tough. He had to be. Serving with No. 2 Commando, he lost both legs penetrating a minefield. With companions, visiting London, he met wartime commandos at a commando pub. Reunion was instant. Seventy-eight British commandos visited Israel. As a result, 1,706 new trees will be planted in that country in the "Forest of Heroes", one tree for each commando killed and named on the roll of honour.

In many places in the world, memorials stand witness to actions by commandos. It seemed only fitting that Scotland should have a memorial to the commandos too. Scotland, where the commandos had been trained.

So, on a hill in the heart of Lochaber, a memorial was raised. Three gigantic bronze figures, in cap-comforters and S.V. climbing boots, facing up to the elements the way they had stoically followed their leaders, undaunted and unflinching.

Her Majesty, the Queen Mother, had unveiled the memorial. Some of the words she had spoken remain firmly embedded in my mind. Words to the effect that, "Courage and bravery are not the prerogative of any one section of the community—but are to be found in great abundance in Britain."

There was a time, in 1940, in Britain, when these isles lay besieged. Bombs fell from the heavens to explode on cities. Streets suffered flame and fire, homes were reduced to rubble. Men, women and children stood desolate and bewildered. Suddenly, out of darkness, cool, calm, confident, cocky commandos, with consummate cheek, struck back into German-occupied territory. Retribution, the day of reckoning for the Nazis, was here.

I sat on a huge flat stone on the hillside beneath the memorial. Comfortable in the kilt, black brogues on home-spun, natural-coloured stockings and wearing a cool white shirt, I relaxed and let the peace of this place flow through my veins, draining pressure away and leaving me content to dream.

The scene before me unfolded. The Great Glen stretching away to Inverlochy, Fort William and Ben Nevis. The noise of the coach drawing in to the lay-by interrupted my thoughts. I turned my head in annoyance and saw the party of people alight. I hoped they would not laugh and chatter in loud voices. But they were moving quietly and whispering in undertones. One of them was dressed in clerical grey and had on the dog-collar of a minister. A church outing perhaps. I turned back to the panoramic view, unconsciously following the unseeing eyes of the three bronze figures above me.

Suddenly I heard the silence, as if the world had been stilled by an unseen hand. It was queer that, hearing the silence . . .

Cautiously, I glanced round.

The church party was gathered together, heads bowed, in front of the memorial. Then I heard her voice, a contralto deep and clear, break the hush.

She began to hum a tune, giving the key. Soprano, base and tenor followed like the prelude to an overture. Softly at first, the tune was taken up by the others, gathering strength till the notes became words swelling to a crescendo. The words drifted upwards to curl and linger about the three "men" on the hill, and to die away caught by the fine air spiralling towards the clouds. The clouds were floating fleetingly across the blue to converge on Ben Nevis, "Beinn Nimheis", the "Hill of Heaven".

A great beam of light sheered through, spotlighting the peak. The Ben was snow-capped, priest-like, glittering, robed in sunshine. Deep-blue shadows on either side concealed its power of life and death.

I recognized the tune. It was a great favourite with my mother and father at home in Paisley. It was a great favourite in many homes. I listened, stirred and enthralled as the voices echoed and re-echoed down the Great Glen, "I to the hills will lift mine eyes."

That was what the three men on the hill above Spean in Lochaber had done. That was what they were doing now. It seemed a good thing to do—so I did that!

# Regiments, Corps and Other Formations from which the Officers and Men of the 1st Commando Brigade Were Drawn

Royal Horse Guards
Royal Dragoons
8th Hussars
Lovat Scouts
Royal Armoured Corps
Royal Tank Regiment
City of London Yeomanry
Royal Regiment of Artillery (Field Heavy Anti-aircraft. Coastal and Searchlights)
11th Hussars
12th Lancers
Corps of Royal Engineers
Royal Corps of Signals
Grenadier Guards
Irish Guards
Buffs
King's Regiment (including the King's Liverpool Irish)
Royal Fusiliers
Devonshire Regiment
Somerset Light Infantry
East Yorkshire Regiment
Green Howards
Duke of Cornwall's Light Infantry
Hampshire Regiment
Dorsetshire Regiment
Royal Welsh Fusiliers
Life Guards
Scots Greys

King's Dragoon Guards
Inniskilling Dragoon Guards
9th Lancers
Berkshire Yeomanry
Lanarkshire Yeomanry
Ayrshire Yeomanry
Coldstream Guards
Scots Guards
Royal Scots
Royal Warwickshire Regiment
Royal Norfolk Regiment
Suffolk Regiment
West Yorkshire Regiment
Bedfordshire and Hertfordshire Regiment
Lancashire Fusiliers
King's Own Scottish Borderers
The Cameronians (Scottish Rifles)
Gloucestershire Regiment
East Lancashire Regiment
Black Watch
Oxfordshire and Buckinghamshire Light Infantry
Loyal Regiment
Welsh Regiment
Essex Regiment
Sherwood Foresters
Royal Berkshire Regiment
King's Own Yorkshire Light Infantry

King's Royal Rifle Corps
Highland Light Infantry
Royal Ulster Rifles
Royal Army Service Corps
Royal Army Ordnance Corps
Liaison Regiment
Free French No 10 Commando
No 45 Royal Marine Commando
Royal Inniskilling Fusiliers
Worcestershire Regiment
East Surrey Regiment
Border Regiment
South Staffordshire Regiment

South Lancashire Regiment
Queen's Own Royal West Kent
   Regiment
King's Shropshire Light Infantry
Durham Light Infantry
Liverpool Scottish (Queen's Own
   Cameron Highlanders)
Rifle Brigade
Royal Army Medical Corps
Royal Army Dental Corps
Honourable Artillery Company
U.S. Rangers (attached)

# Details of Craft

**Dory**   Approximately 20 feet overall. Beam 5 feet 4 inches; depth 2 feet 2 inches; weight 6 cwt; capacity 1.9 long tons (8 to 10 men); oars 9 feet 6 inches.

**Goatley**   Collapsible boat with wooden bottom and green canvas sides – 11 feet 6 inches overall. Beam 4 feet 6 inches; depth 1 foot 9 inches; weight 2 cwt. Carried 7 men, 6 paddling. Two men could assemble it in 1½ minutes.

**LCA**   Landing Craft Assault. Of 13 tons displacement when loaded; 35 troops with 800 lb of equipment. Range 50–80 miles. Operational speed 7 knots. Wooden craft of 41 feet. Crew of 4. Protected with armour to craft's well sides and to side decking. Two engines.

**LCIs**   Landing Craft Infantry (small). Designed for long-distance raids. 110 long tons displacement; assault force 6 officers and 96 ORs. Wooden craft with crew of 17. Petrol engines fitted with silencers. Assault force landed down two bow gangways. Had range of 700 miles and speed of 12½ knots. Armament two 20-mm and two Lewis guns.

**LCP**   Landing Craft Personnel. Carried assault force of 25, landing by jumping down from high prow. Wooden craft 36 feet 8 inches long. Range approximately 120 miles at 9 to 11 knots. For raiding, had cockpit forward of troop well with canvas hood to give protection from weather.

**LCT**   Landing Craft Tank. Steel, carried approx. 150 tons. Tanks landed from ramp. Often used to ferry troops etc.

**LVT**   Landing Vehicles Tracked. Armoured troop-carriers designed with tracks that paddled across water and over mud. Air-cooled 200 hp engine gave land range of 150 miles with a max. speed of 25 m.p.h. and, over water, 75 miles with a speed of 5.4 knots.

# Index